Gardens
Are for People

Gardens Are for People

Thomas D. Church

Grace Hall
Michael Laurie

SECOND EDITION

McGRAW-HILL BOOK COMPANY
New York   St. Louis   San Francisco   Auckland
Bogotá   Hamburg   Johannesburg   London
Madrid   Mexico   Montreal   New Delhi
Panama   São Paulo   Singapore
Sydney   Tokyo   Toronto

Library of Congress Cataloging in Publication Data

Church, Thomas Dolliver.
  Gardens are for people.

  Includes index.
  1. Gardens—Design.   2. Landscape gardening.
I. Hall, Grace (Grace M.)   II. Laurie, Michael.
III. Title.
SB473.C5   1983   712′.6   82-14000

ISBN 0-07-010844-7

1234567890   HALHAL   898765432

ISBN 0-07-010844-7

*The editors for this book were Joan Zseleczky and Carolyn Nagy,
the designer was Naomi Auerbach, and the production supervisor
was Teresa F. Leaden. It was set in Electra
by Progressive Typographers, Inc.
Printed and bound by Halliday Lithograph, Inc.*

Dedicated to Betsy, my wife, without whom . . .

ABOUT THE AUTHOR

THOMAS D. CHURCH *was a distinguished landscape architect whose reputation and influence were worldwide. He changed the profession through his writing and photography, and through collaboration with the best architects. Church was educated in the 1920s at the University of California, Berkeley, at the Harvard Graduate School of Design, and in Europe on a Sheldon Traveling Fellowship. Until his retirement in 1977, he practiced landscape architecture in San Francisco. His contribution to the Exposition Gardens on Treasure Island, California, in 1940 was much acclaimed. For his creative achievements, he received awards from the American Institute of Architects, the American Society of Landscape Architects, the American Horticultural Society, plus a fellowship from the American Academy of Arts and Sciences.*

GRACE HALL, assistant to the late Thomas D. Church, and MICHAEL LAURIE, *Professor of Landscape Architecture, the University of California at Berkeley, are the editors of this book.*

Contents

THOMAS CHURCH, 1975

Photograph by Carolyn Caddes

Preface

Thomas Church began his professional career in San Francisco in the 1930s, after conventional beaux arts training at the University of California in Berkeley and the Harvard Graduate School of Design. The timing coincided with a rapidly changing social context in California and a revolution in art and architecture on an international scale. By the 1950s Church had become one of the leading landscape architects in the United States, working on large commercial and institutional projects with eminent architects of the modern movement, including Eero Saarinen and Edward Durell Stone. But the bulk of his practice was on a domestic scale, and it was on garden design that his reputation was based.

His sensitivity to historical precedent, the environment of California, and the changing lifestyle and values of his clients, together with a mind receptive to new concepts in art and architecture, brought to his early work unique forms and new spatial qualities. His best gardens seem to be natural products of time and place and reflect the changes in taste and attitude already growing and requiring to be given form. These gardens not only fall into the realm of fine art but also represent an important milestone in the evolution of the modern garden and landscape architecture.

Locally, Church associated with young modern architects of the Bay Area (William Wurster, Gardner Dailey, Ernest Born, and others), and together, for adventurous clients, they produced integrated houses and gardens based on the new aesthetic and designed for California living. The ratio of house to garden was frequently high, and the automobile further contributed to a reduction of usable garden space for the average home owner.

Church's designs to accommodate the increasing use of small gardens by families and the need to reduce maintenance included hard surfaces and ground-cover planting, screens to separate areas and provide privacy, techniques and illusions to increase apparent size, and shapes suited to topography, function, and upkeep. The combination of this relatively new design problem, the small garden, with the new approach to form resulted in a major breakthrough for landscape architecture. While the garden satisfied all practical criteria, the central axis was abandoned in favor of a multiplicity of viewpoints. Simple planes and flowing lines, texture and color, space and form were manipulated in a manner reminiscent of the cubist painters. Not only did the gardens which Church designed in the late 1930s look different, they also represented a new and improved way of dealing with landscape design on any scale. Each design derived form and uniqueness from careful appraisal and analysis of the site, from the architecture of the house, and from the client's personality and preferences.

Historical precedent was not rejected by Church. In fact, his work drew strength from an appreciation of good design of whatever age and an understanding of the present as it evolves out of the past. He had an exceptional ability to translate a client's requirements into a logical and intelligent plan, which at the same time derived specific quality from the surrounding environment. His deep understanding of the California landscape and its tradition and history and of the lifestyle and values of his clients makes his work, albeit for a small section of society, a logical part of its evolution.

Thomas Church had an enormous influence on modern landscape architecture as it evolved in the postwar years in the United States. He wrote prolifically for the architectural and garden magazines and in 1955 published *Gardens Are for People*, followed in 1969 by *Your Private World*. *Gardens Are for People* is an impressive and charming book about landscape design; it is considered a milestone in garden literature and, as one newspaper reviewer remarked, " . . . to read it is to take a course in landscape gardening."

Tommy Church was referred to as a genius, a practical man, the guiding light of landscape architecture. In addition, his office nurtured many young landscape architects who are now leaders in the profession. In recognition of his contribution he received the Fine Arts Medal of the American Institute of Architects (1951), the Gold Medal of the American Society of Landscape Architects (1976), the Gold Medal of the New York Architectural League (1953), the Oakleigh Thorne Medal from the Garden Club of America (1969) and a Fellowship of the American Academy of Arts and Sciences (1978).

This new edition of *Gardens Are for People* was conceived by Mr. Church prior to his death in August 1978. Colleagues had, for several years, urged him to initiate a second edition; it was a project for which he had enormous enthusiasm, but unfortunately, because of the demands of an active practice, and latterly because of illness, he never completed it. However, to the end, like a true designer, Tommy Church, who had always equated work with pleasure and life itself, worked on the book with his assistant, Grace Hall, selecting photographs and making notes for the new edition.

The present volume represents the culmination of these and other efforts to bring together an up-to-date record of the work and theory of Thomas D. Church, landscape architect, 1902–1978. The original text of his book has been somewhat reorganized and, where appropriate, supplemented with material from other sources. Some of the gardens in the 1955 edition have been eliminated or are now illustrated with more recent photography. While gardens completed since 1955 predominate, the selection (from over 2000 gardens) represents work from every stage of Church's practice. Many of the photographs are published for the first time.

Although his work was of a particular genre, Mr. Church's approach to design is timeless and of general application at all levels and scales of landscape architecture; thus, in addition to providing a record of the work of a distinguished landscape architect, it is hoped that this new edition of *Gardens Are for People*, with its fine photography, plans, and sketches (many from Church's hand) and concise text, will be found useful by students of all ages.

Michael Laurie
SAN FRANCISCO

Foreword

To voice the thoughts of those of us fortunate enough to have had our lives touched by this unique, sensitive man, certainly a genius in his field, the eloquent recognition given Thomas Church by the American Institute of Architects is reproduced here. Printed on parchment, the award sums up, in comparatively few words, the enormous contribution he made to the profession of landscape architecture.

We have been fortunate in having access to all of the author's writing on the subject of landscape design, including his two books and many magazine articles. The text of the first five chapters draws largely on the original edition of *Gardens Are for People* and is supplemented here and there with excerpts from the other sources. The Church office files were an invaluable archive of plans, and Mr. Church's own drawings have been used wherever appropriate. They have been specially prepared, and most are seen publicly for the first time.

During the early years of Mr. Church's practice, many young landscape architects entered his office before progressing to highly successful practices of their own. Among them were Lawrence Halprin, Casey Kawamoto, Theodore Osmundson, Robert Royston, Jack Stafford, and Jack Valette. It is impossible to mention by name all who have worked on the Thomas Church garden designs: the associates in his office, the contractors who built the gardens, the craftsmen whose specialized touch is seen throughout, the gardeners whose continual care brought them to maturity. He would be the first to acknowledge their many skills and contributions.

We are particularly indebted to certain people, whose names belong in these pages, for their great assistance during the preparation of this book: Mrs. Thomas Church, for her knowledgeable comments on the gardens and valued advice and involvement; Morley Baer, Margaret Blair, and Rondal Partridge, friends of Mr. Church, for their beautiful photographic contributions; Carolyn Caddes, for her many travels to catch gardens at their peak of perfection and looking their best for her photography; Lisa Guthrie, Walter Guthrie, and Samuel Ciofalo, former associates of the Church office, for their superb professional advice throughout the book; the management of Longwood Gardens, for permission to reproduce their photographs of the finished designs; Pam-Anela Messenger, for her generous contribution of her garden photography, permission to use information from her thesis on the work of Thomas Church, and extensive research that has been invaluable in preparing descriptive notes on the gardens; Mrs. Maynard Parker, who has given us permission to use a large number of her late husband's fine photographs; and William Sears and Minot Eaton, for arranging a daylong tour in Santa Barbara for the purpose of photographing the gardens there.

In assembling the photographs for his book, every effort has been made to acknowledge the individual photographers' beautiful visual portrayals of his garden designs. In some cases the pictures have been in his office files for many years, and it is possible that a credit may have been inadvertently overlooked. If this should be so, it will be corrected in a future edition. Photographs not otherwise credited were taken by Thomas Church.

Last, but certainly not least, we thank the owners of these beautiful gardens, the kind people who planted, pruned, and swept, then graciously opened their homes and permitted us to enter and photograph their private worlds.

It was always Thomas Church's wish to design gardens for people to enjoy. As he said, "Gardens *are* for people." It is hoped that the second edition of his book will be enjoyed not only by people who live within sight of his gardens but by people far afield who will get to know them from the descriptions and photography in the book.

To quote from Ecclesiastes 12, " . . . of making many books there is no end. . . . "

Grace Hall
SAN FRANCISCO

ANNO DOMINI MCMLI

THE AMERICAN INSTITUTE OF ARCHITECTS

TAKES PLEASURE IN HONORING A MASTER OF THE
ART OF LANDSCAPE ARCHITECTURE. FOR THE GREAT
HAPPINESS GIVEN IN THE JOYS OF PEACEFUL POSSES-
SIONS. FOR THE OPPORTUNITIES THROUGH HIS DESIGNS
OF GRACIOUS LIFE UNDER SUN AND RAIN IN CLOSURES
WHERE FLOWERS AND TREES AND WIDE TERRACES
BRING NEW MEANINGS NOT ONLY TO THOSE WHO,
HAPPILY, LIVE WITHIN THEM, BUT ALSO AS INSPIRA-
TIONS TO HIS COLLEAGUES AND TO ARCHITECTS WHOSE
WORK THESE DESIGNS SO GENEROUSLY ADORN. THE
FINE ARTS MEDAL IS AWARDED TO

THOMAS DOLLIVER CHURCH

IN RECOGNITION OF AN OUTSTANDING ABILITY IN THE
CREATION OF BEAUTY. IN THE GRACEFUL WEAVING OF THE
GLORIES OF NATURE INTO THE LIVES OF MEN . BRINGING
TO THEM THE PEACE WHICH FLOWS IN PLENTY FROM
THE SPRINGS WATERING THE GARDENS OF THE EARTH.

SECRETARY

PRESIDENT

Design

THOMAS CHURCH, 1971

Photograph by Glenn Christiansen, courtesy of Sunset Magazine

Introduction

There are a number of phrases in use which express in general terms our longing to live *in* our site, such as "the integration of the house and garden," "indoor-outdoor living," and "the relation of shelter to land."

Some years ago a garden magazine, throwing caution to the winds, published an article called "The Wedding of the House and Garden."

It is not a new idea. The Egyptians planned their houses and gardens together. The Romans knew all about it. The Greeks had a word for it; and the Renaissance Italians developed it to a fine art. They had outside living rooms, dining rooms, corridors, and entrance halls. They borrowed line and materials from the house; and they borrowed foliage, shade, fruit, flowers, and the play of water from nature. It was a subtle compromise. The struggle of forces—the light touch of nature and the heavy hand of man—left no trace of incongruity. The garden was a transitional stage saving them from the embarrassment of stepping from their house to nature in the raw.

In the great renaissance of gardening in Italy, designers were often faced with steep and difficult sites, where great ingenuity was required to relate one level to another. Their ramps and stairways often incorporated pools and fountains, highly embellished with ornament and sculpture.

The terrace, in all periods of gardening, and whether called atrium, close, promenade, or lanai, has been an obviously man-made part of the garden. It has been used to extend the architectural lines of the house and supplement the activities of the occupants. Today, the "terrace" area is for outdoor living.

In Pompeii, the terrace was an inside court, surrounded by the rooms of the house. It was simple and severe, cooled by the sound of water and removed from the noises of the street.

The enclosed court was used throughout the Middle Ages when it was unwise to venture outside the walls. In Spain, as the patio, it reached its highest development as a decorative adjunct to the house. Here they had sun or shade, fresh air, cooling fountains, fruit trees, colorful vines and potted plants, and above all, seclusion and privacy.

In the large formal gardens developed after the 16th century, the terrace was an intermediate stop between the house and a vast complex of formal parterres. The gardens were large—grandeur and great scale were the order of the day. They could hold large crowds; Louis XIV gave a party on the terraces of Versailles for 3000 people which lasted for three days.

The Chinese style laid its delicate hand on all the arts in the eighteenth century. It influenced the English school of landscape gardening and sent landscapers scurrying back to Nature for inspiration. The waving line was proclaimed a true line of beauty, forgetting that a straight line is the best foil for the graceful curves in flower and plant.

Nature was out-natured. Faked dead trees and crumbling ruins were added to heighten the effect of natural decay. Lancelot ("Capability") Brown (1716–1783) constructed a river across an estate which he considered so beautiful that he cried, "Alas! The Thames will never forgive me!" Terraces were plowed under, the incomparable Elizabethan flower gardens were discovered to be unnatural. Trim Tudor gardens, with their borders of "sweet smelling herbes," were out of style, and many of them were destroyed before the wave had spent its strength.

Humphry Repton followed a few years later, gathered up the pieces, and, putting them together in logical order, made Nature a full partner in the humanized landscape. But the generations of smaller home owners in the next century, who attempted to recreate these natural scenes on their own small plots of ground, were misled. Nature is not easily transplanted to one's back yard.

This eighteenth-century rediscovery of nature in the garden and the nineteenth-century adaptation of its principles became our immediate heritage.

The nineteenth century saw the glorification of the specimen plant and the introduction of horticultural rarities throughout the world. (Douglas discovered the sequoia, and also the fir which bears his name, and sent them back to England; today you see them all over Europe.)

Americans discovered a thousand varieties and, liking the new and rare, tried them all—on the front lawn.

*Residence of Dr. C. A. Kirkpatrick
Redwood City, Cal.*

Our Heritage

From centuries of man's attempt to control and beautify his
surroundings, we inherit a vast knowledge of botany, horticulture, and
the uses to which it has pleased him to put the flowers and plants at
his disposal.

He has tried many things—from a complete and rigid control of all
plant forms, with flowers providing a delicate pattern of embroidery, to
a free and untrammelled expression of undisturbed nature. All have
served some purpose in relating him to his times and to his
surroundings.

Today we take the best from these two schools of thought (once
bitter enemies)—the formal and the informal—the symmetrical and
the picturesque—the geometric and the natural—the classic and the
romantic.

We still have a strong tendency to control our surroundings, but in
our gardens we want plants, by their structure and poetry, to suggest
the fine melancholy we expect in nature. Thus do we borrow from the
past.

The Columbian Exposition in 1893 ushered in the greatest wave of
"copyism" since England discovered Palladio. Our countryside was
soon teeming with Italian villas, Moorish castles, and French manor
houses. Architects and landscapers scurried on the Grand Tour with
their rulers and notebooks. While this resulted in some fine
reproductions of old-world gardens, it proved the hollowness of
imitation without reason.

The 1925 Exposition des Arts Décoratifs in Paris, with architecture
and garden design showing the influence of streamlining and abstract

art, and the Exposition Internationale of 1937, which included glass and steel pavilions, new materials, modern sculpture, and broad-scale planting in the gardens, were brave attempts to break through the bonds of this eclecticism and establish a new order.

The rising tide of revolt went to excesses, as all revolutions must, and Art Moderne strangled in the mesh of its own steel tubing and alternating squares of colored pebbles and violas. The gardens of the period became the attempts of a three-dimensional art to reproduce the two-dimensional compositions of the modern painters. "Modern" was a battle cry which degenerated into a style and, finally, into a nasty word. Designers seemed to be annoyed, rather than grateful, that anyone had preceded them.

Today we are facing the end of a century which promises a clearer understanding of man's relationship to his environment. "Modern" can be revived as an honest word when we realize that modernism is not a goal but a broad highway.

Garden Design Today

In any age of reason, it is the owner who finally decides the size of his garden and the purposes for which it shall be used.

The garden owner is being constructive about his problems when he analyzes what he really wants as disassociated from what tradition may have convinced him he ought to have. Assuming he stays within the vague bounds of good taste, he can have just what he wants.

There are no mysterious "musts," no set rules, no finger of shame pointed at the gardener who doesn't follow an accepted pattern.

Landscaping is not a complex and difficult art to be practiced only by high priests. It is logical, down-to-earth, and aimed at making your plot of ground produce exactly what you want and need from it.

What do you want and need? Take a long and earnest look into your crystal ball. You will see that economic pressures have reduced the average house to a minimum and that the functions of the house have spilled over into the garden. You will see that you need additional space for lounging, eating, and entertaining; you will see that your closets and garage are bulging with a miscellany of personal belongings, tools, play equipment, ad infinitum, which the site must provide for.

Yet it must also perform its primary function of being a garden in the true sense of providing trees and flowers, fruits and vegetables; a place where man can recapture his affinity with the soil, if only on Saturday afternoons. It must be a green oasis where memories of his bumper-to-bumper ride from work will be erased.

We're all different; and our gardens and what we expect our land to do for us will vary as much as our demands and our personalities. No one can design intelligently for you unless he knows what you need, what you want, and what you are like. If you won't tell, he will have to guess.

It's just as wrong to give an owner who is not an ambitious gardener a combination of natural plantings requiring expert knowledge and care as it is to give a real "green thumb" gardener a garden with no soil to dig in.

The direction in which to move will be determined by the desires of the people who expect to find happiness in their gardens. Happiness will come by adding as much beauty and by eliminating as many irritations as possible within the limits of the problem. The limits of the problem will be the restrictions and opportunities of the site and the ability of the owner and designer to overcome or make use of them.

Gardens Are for People is not a book primarily concerned with the planting of a garden, nor does it attempt to explain all the great underlying principles of garden design. Many excellent books have covered these fields and I have quoted freely from them.

It is, rather, a garden tour, with some comment in passing. It shows what people wanted and how we helped them to get it, or if they didn't know, how we helped them to decide. I hope that much of what is shown is universal in its application and will vary only as it is affected by local climates and practices.

To weigh, advise, interpret, integrate, and come up with some answers beyond the ability and imagination of the layman is the role of the landscape architect.

Thomas Church

2

The Site Affects Design
(and Site Improvements Affect the Budget)

The perfect site is on slightly rising ground with large, healthy trees, a fine view, or a beautiful background of foliage; it has deep, rich topsoil and is oriented to be out of the wind but to catch all the sunshine. As long as we're dreaming, we might as well add that it is near schools, churches, and shops and that all utilities are already at the property line. If you find it, buy it.

If you're going to look for property, take your architect and landscape architect along—they are qualified to advise you. The landscape architect can measure your requirements and your budget against the probable cost of developing the property. Maybe the trees are either poor varieties or in bad condition; maybe it's covered with obnoxious weeds which would be almost impossible to eradicate. There may be indications of poor drainage, heavy clay soil, erosion, or exposure that should influence your decision. If you're looking at the property on a hot summer day and find it lush and cool, you may forget it's a north slope with no sun from October to March.

Most people start out with a budget. The only hope of staying within it is to avoid guesswork as much as you can and to know all possible costs before you commit yourself. To the average layman the headings are simple: the lot, the house, the furniture, the garden (it will be done gradually later). The garden allowance covers only soil preparation, plants, and lawns.

But—ever hear of site improvements? They're seldom included in the first budget, and yet they're real costs. Aside from special conditions imposed by the site or the client's whims, they consist of tree clearing and rough grading, boundary fences, entrance road and

". . . above all, it should be healthful, not situate in a low or marshy ground, because of the Corruption caused there by the infectious Breath of Venomous Animals which breed there and occasion many Noxious Humours and Distempers; and that the House be not turned to the South or West, because Heat weakens the Body and Cold strengthens it."
VITRUVIUS, *Ten Books of Architecture*, 1st century B.C.

parking, additional leveling and fine grading after the house is built, retaining walls, drainage system, hose bibbs and sprinklers, garden structures (toolhouse, bathhouse, extra storage), screen fences within the garden, and garden lighting. Most of them should be done before you move in. On a simple, flat lot they may not strain your budget, but on tough terrain they may cost as much as the house itself.

Don't cross your fingers and hope the bids will come in low. They won't. The things you will have to eliminate may be the things you want most.

Find out where you're going before you start. It is possible, even desirable, to use the disadvantages of your lot to your own advantage—in other words, to work with the land, its natural character and substance, rather than against it.

Orientation Should Affect Design

Look carefully at your site before you sigh and place the house square to the property lines with the living room on the street and the kitchen and garage at the rear. A problem which confronts many an owner of a contemporary home is the relation of the house to the street, particularly when that is the best orientation for garden living.

Rooms can go anywhere you want them for the right amount of sun at the right time of year. Wings of the house can protect garden areas. If you want large areas of glass, be wary of south and west exposures. No amount of overhang will shield the glass from the late summer sun. Your pleasure will be diminished if you have to close heavy drapes at four o'clock.

Since we can't all have the famous house which turns with the seasons, get the best possible orientation for the house and the garden areas.

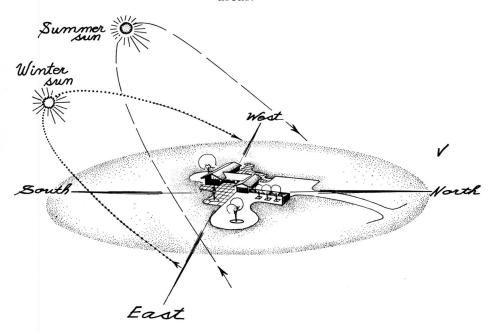

An Island Garden in Maine

This house and garden, built in the mid-1970s, magnificently sited on the coast of Maine, required no visual distraction from the view of neighboring islands and out to the Atlantic.

Maintenance is kept to a minimum with a terrace of stone native to the area. Spring- and summer-blooming flowers are grown in colorful pots and urns, easily transported inside to escape the rigors of winter in the northeastern United States.

Photographs by Margaret Blair

Topography Affects Design
On a Hillside, Saratoga, California

The site forced this garden along a narrow ridge.

This country site in Saratoga lies along the top of a rocky ridge with fine views in all directions.

The amenities the owners wanted—a pool, roses, fruit trees, and vegetables—are strung out along the only level area. The rose garden and vegetable beds are raised, not only for neatness and convenience, but because they are built on a rock base. It proved to be a more economical way of getting sufficient topsoil than excavating and draining the garden planting space.

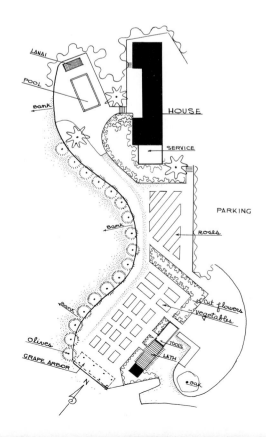

Placing the House

The most obvious place to put the house is not always the right one. If there is only a small area of flat land, you'll be tempted to use it for the house. It probably should be saved for arrival, parking, or garden. Houses can be built on a slope, but it means a lot of grading and walls later when you try to get enough flat land for the areas you need around the house. Is there one particular spot on the property that seems just right in every way? Have you picnicked there and found it idyllic?

Have you spent long winter evenings planning a house there? Has it occurred to you that if you build your house there the spot will be gone? Maybe that's where your garden should be.

Ask yourself these questions:

Do you want morning light in the bedrooms?

In a hot climate, do you like a north kitchen?

If the dominant view is to the west—and you want the main rooms to have that view—what are you doing about controlling the afternoon sunshine?

Is the house placed to allow adequate arrival and parking space? Do you know the minimum turning radius for your car? Can you turn in and out of your garage without breaking your elbows?

These and many other special problems need to be recognized and solved in a preliminary way before you go ahead.

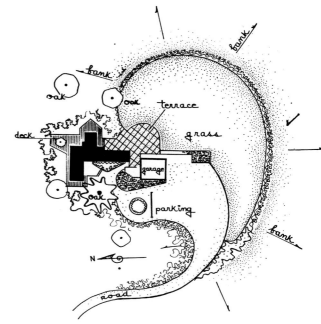

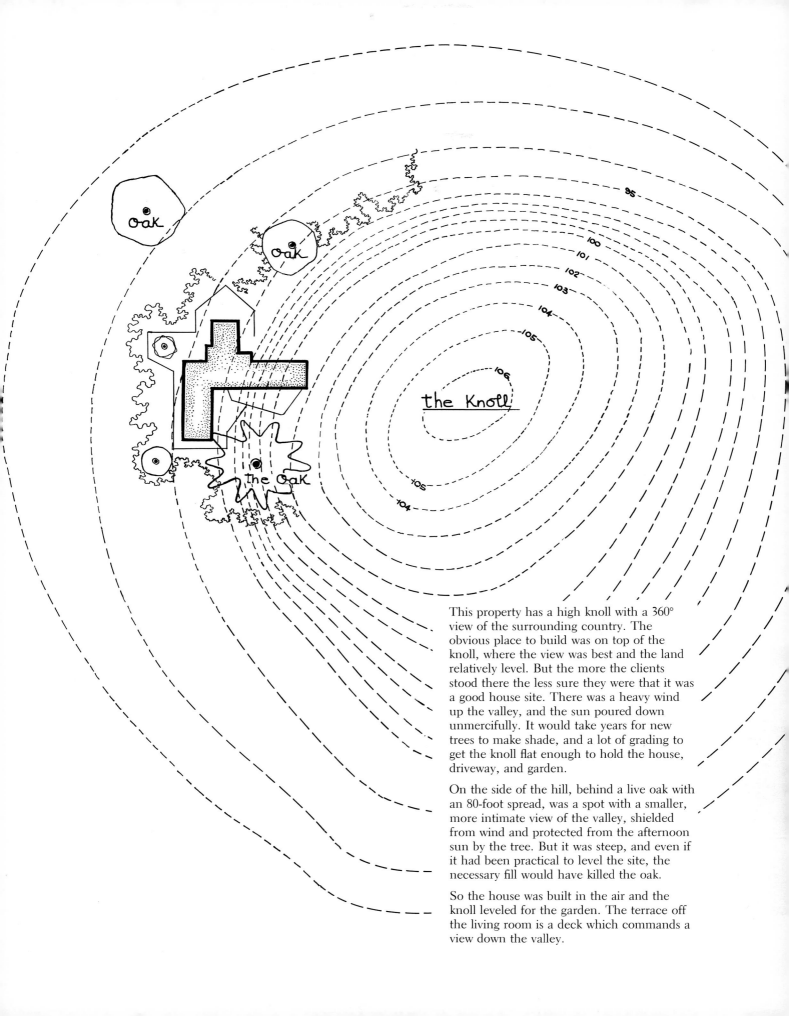

Oak

Oak

the Knoll

the Oak

95

100

101

102

103

104

105

106

105

105

104

This property has a high knoll with a 360°
view of the surrounding country. The
obvious place to build was on top of the
knoll, where the view was best and the land
relatively level. But the more the clients
stood there the less sure they were that it was
a good house site. There was a heavy wind
up the valley, and the sun poured down
unmercifully. It would take years for new
trees to make shade, and a lot of grading to
get the knoll flat enough to hold the house,
driveway, and garden.

On the side of the hill, behind a live oak with
an 80-foot spread, was a spot with a smaller,
more intimate view of the valley, shielded
from wind and protected from the afternoon
sun by the tree. But it was steep, and even if
it had been practical to level the site, the
necessary fill would have killed the oak.

So the house was built in the air and the
knoll leveled for the garden. The terrace off
the living room is a deck which commands a
view down the valley.

BEFORE

"One of the melancholy appendages observable in the pleasure grounds of the past century is a long lawn without cattle."

HUMPHRY REPTON,
The Theory and Practice of Landscape Gardening, 1803

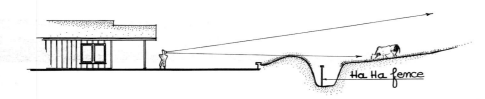

Ha Ha fence

AFTER

Photograph by Carolyn Caddes

How to Enjoy Land You Don't Own

In eighteenth-century England, cattle grazed on the public lands and were a constant and necessary part of every landscape.

To keep them out of their pleasure grounds and still be able to see the flowing meadows and woods, landowners constructed a ditch with a fence at the bottom, called a "fosse" or "ha-ha." This allowed the eye to move uninterruptedly over the pastoral landscape and to accept all it saw as its own.

This home owner doesn't want cows in his swimming pool but, like the eighteenth-century Englishman, he likes them in his landscape. A fence was necessary, but he didn't want to see it. If he planted it out, he would lose the cows and the view.

So the fence was lowered into a ditch at the property line, the lawn rolls up to foreshorten against the meadow, and the nearby cow and the distant hills appear to be a part of the property.

Someone else feeds and milks the cows. This home owner looks at them.

Large black coils which were installed years later, on the side of the ditch and thus hidden from view, are used for solar-heating the pool.

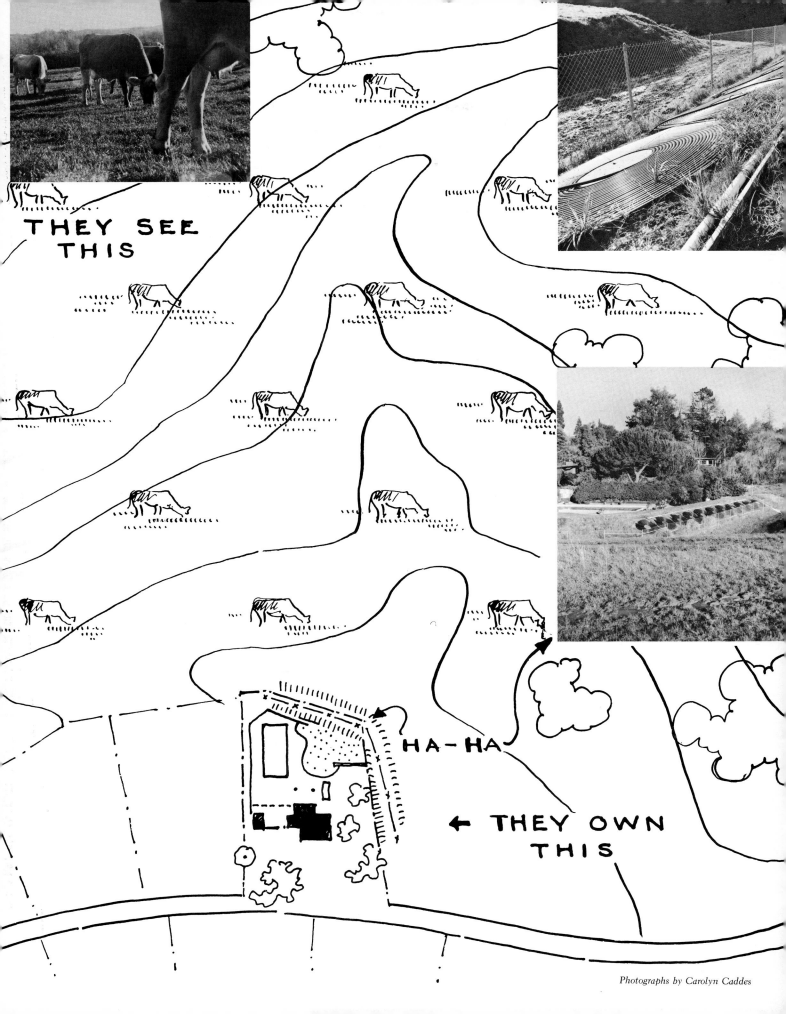

THEY SEE
THIS

HA-HA

← THEY OWN
THIS

Photographs by Carolyn Caddes

Views Affect Design

Distant views of mountains and water, intimate views of hills and woods, views over cities at night, all have an endless fascination for people. To get them they will search for penthouses and hilltops, install elevators, move mountains, clear forests, and build decks.

Put as few obstacles and diverting lines as possible between you and your view if you want it to retain all its drama. The eye is fickle and easily distracted.

A curved line against a view presents the least irritation. In the garden at right, a low planting separates the lawn from the slope.

Photograph by Maynard L. Parker

Photograph by Maynard L. Parker

A million-dollar view of San Francisco's Golden Gate was just around the corner—of the neighbor's house.

A deck was constructed across the living room, along the house next door and 40 feet above the ground, to a "crow's nest." From it, the owners see the Golden Gate—and, for the first time, the rear of their own house.

The living room windows, facing north, were changed to a glass wall with doors opening onto the deck.

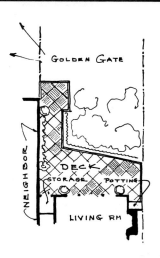

Photograph by Carolyn Caddes

Slope Affects Design

You may apply the theory of visual appropriation of property not your own if you live next to a park or golf course, orchard or meadow.

Skip the first impulse to enclose yourself with screen planting and high walls. Instead, look out at the neighboring property. Someone else is maintaining it and paying the taxes; you're enjoying it.

If your lawn can roll so that it foreshortens against the view and the surrounding landscape, you'll have the most for your money.

When the line of mowed grass is carried over the slope, the eye does not see where the lawn meets the natural ground.

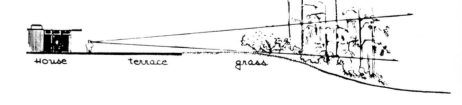

Do Fence Me In

A problem which confronts many an owner
of a contemporary home is the relation of the
house to the street, particularly when that is
the best orientation for garden living.
Sometimes this is not controllable, because
of either regulations or property boundaries.

The home pictured here had such a problem.
When the house was completed the owners
found that their living room with its
expansive glass walls faced the street and was
exposed to the view of all passersby and to
the neighbors across the street. A 6-foot
sapling fence was the solution. By continuing
the terrace area as a wooded platform, to
save filling around the trees, a protected area
was created. It is shaded during the day and
lighted at night, and from the street nobody
knows it's there. From inside, the picket
fence encloses the view, focusing attention
on the garden, and building a deck through
and around the trees made a pleasant and
informal living area.

Photographs by Emelie Danielson Nicholson

Trees Affect Design

Trees provide a setting for many a garden vista (into the garden, toward a view, back to the house).

The shape of the trunk, the curve of a branch, the texture of the foliage, the pattern of the shade may influence your whole design and may determine the shape of your terrace—where you locate the house—or whether you even buy the property.

This Chinese elm was probably stepped on when it was young, yet it has grown into a graceful, multistemmed tree which panels the view without cutting it in two.

In the intimate and humanized landscape, trees become the greatest single element linking us visually and emotionally with our surroundings. Other manifestations of Nature—great rocks, deserts, moors, torrents, hurricanes—stir us, fill us with awe, make us afraid or humble, but a tree we understand and can allow to become part of us. It's no wonder that when we first think of a garden we think of a tree.

You should always make very sure that the tree you were thinking of removing cannot in fact be saved. After all, it took Nature anywhere from ten to three hundred years to get that tree in its current shape; you should carefully consider it before you kill it in twenty minutes. Consider pruning before chopping down; it is possible to both keep the tree and reveal the view it supposedly hides.

On the other hand, some trees have got to go. It's sad, but there it is. The most important thing is still the total home and garden environment—whether it's a comfortable and enjoyable environment as well as a beautiful one. The aesthetic combination of form and function is still the governing factor. If a tree is choking your house or yard, by all means get rid of it.

Because trees have such a feeling of permanence, such a natural stability, everything around them looks more natural, in tune with the landscape and the world. The right trees provide instant serenity—something, in this modern world, which cannot be cherished too highly.

Photograph by Rondal Partridge

Trees Influence the Placing of the House

Rockbound, windblown, and neglected, this tree seemed hardly worth saving. But we wanted it at the end of the house. It was subjected to blasting; many of its roots were cut, and scaffolding was run through the branches and around it.

But it survived, to appear two years later as you see it.

Never underestimate the value of a handsome tree. Protect it, build your house and garden compositions around it, for it offers you shade, shadow, pattern against the sky, protection over your house, a ceiling over your terrace.

Its situation and structure may determine where the house will be built and be the deciding factors in the size and shape it will take. Its shade permits what is otherwise folly—placing windows into the glare of a western sun.

It is worth everything to be able to see your house through the arch of a tree as shown on the opposite page.

Photograph by Maynard L. Parker

Photograph by Maynard L. Parker

Design Principles

(Utility and Beauty in Garden Design)

Designing a garden for a small lot is not an easy thing to discuss theoretically, for each problem brings its own special restrictions and each owner has a different set of tastes and requirements. Nevertheless certain fundamental principles of good garden design apply equally to all problems, large or small, and if these are well considered the basic ground plan of the garden will be sound. Horticultural excellence in the garden can never compensate for a fundamentally bad layout.

What I am about to say regarding design should not be confused with interpretation of the style of the garden. You may choose whether the garden is to follow the traditional style of the house, whether you are to have an English, Spanish, French or American garden. The same good design underlies all these. Style is a matter of taste, design a matter of principle.

The success of the design will depend largely on these four fundamental principles: unity, which is the consideration of the scheme as a whole, both house and garden; function, which is the relation of the practical service areas to the needs of the household and the relation of the decorative areas to the desires and pleasure of those who use it; simplicity, upon which may rest both the economic and aesthetic success of the layout; and scale, which gives us a pleasant relation of parts to one another.

Unity

Before tackling the problem of laying out the garden, let us look at the house. If you were fortunate enough to consider the relation of the house to the garden area when the house was built, you are off to a head start. Doors will lead from the living rooms of the house to the livable areas in the garden. The house will have been placed on the lot to provide sheltered areas for garden living. House foundations will have been so constructed as to allow cutting or filling of soil where flat areas are needed near the house.

Perhaps your house was built in the days when it was considered unhealthy to be less than 4 feet off the ground, dangerous to have a door come into the house at ground level, or bad taste to be able to walk right out into the garden from the house. If this is true, look the house over carefully. Perhaps a dining room window can be changed to a door. Perhaps a terrace can be built outside the living room, with outdoor furniture and pots, and so with steps on into the garden. If your house is still to be built, dwell at length on this subject. There you have principle number one, ease of access and a feeling of intimacy between house and garden.

Function

On a small lot you are definitely space-bound. You cannot have all the gardens you have clipped from the pages of *House Beautiful* and *Arts and Architecture*, although many people try. The problem is complicated enough with all the things that must be fitted into the limited area. The service arrangements must be considered first, for they are inevitable. First we must get the service requirements into as small an area as they need to function properly. There is the garbage can and tool shed. There should be a space to burn garden rubbish where permitted, then a vegetable garden, and perhaps a dog run. These utilitarian features should be arranged in an orderly and unobtrusive manner. They will find themselves, logically, near the service areas of the house. The remainder of the lot may be devoted to the more decorative units of the garden.

Simplicity

It is not wise to be overambitious in designing the garden. Too many things going on in a small area produces a restless quality which will leave the onlooker dissatisfied. The design is influenced directly by the house. The house dominates the area and must be allowed to dictate the general lines of the garden. The unity of the whole scheme is advanced when the line and material of the house are carried into the garden. A terrace provides a transitional stage between the house and garden as well as adding an outdoor room. Where space is very limited, the whole area may be taken up with the garden terrace. Beware of the illusion that a waving, uncertain line is going to give the boundary a more natural feeling. Nine times out of ten it will seem more artificial than the simple rectangle which follows the lines of the house and property. You have created the garden, just as you have the house, as a frankly man-made thing for your use and enjoyment. It is a little unfair to attempt to prove that Nature has crept slyly over the back fence and done the job for you.

Scale

Last, but most important, is scale. Hard to define, impossible to give hard and fast rules for, it can nevertheless make or break the success of the design. It affects the line and proportion of the garden areas and the height and mass of the planting. Relative scale means the relation of one part of a design to another, and absolute scale means their relation to the human figure. The width of a path, for instance, is influenced both by a person who is to walk along it and by the size of the area through which it passes.

Our first checkup on scale is the relation of our garden area to the facade of the house. A terrace width which we might assume as a neat dimension in itself might prove wholly inadequate in proportion to the size of the house. The dimensions of a garden may not be bad in themselves but may fail in their relation to the size of other areas. When the whole scheme becomes cramped and crowded it may have perfect relative scale but fail in its relation to the human figure. The best general rule to follow is: when in doubt, make it larger. The eye detects a meager dimension more easily than it does a too-generous one.

The Design

It is important that the garden be built around a dominant idea. Do one thing well and let all others be subordinate in scale to this idea. If it be a central grass plot surrounded by a flower border do not clutter the area with miscellaneous planting and garden ornament which will distract the eye and diminish the dramatic effect of the scale of the original conception. Do not be afraid of large paved surfaces on terraces and entrance courts. The scale of these areas and the simplicity of their unbroken lines are an important consideration in the pleasant relation of the garden to the house. Hard, uncompromising lines in the garden can be softened, to almost any extent desired, by planting. Once it is realized that this softening should be done by planting rather than by altering the dominant lines of the floor plan of the garden, you are on your way to a successful garden layout.

We all know completely natural gardens which are the envy of everyone who sees them—steep wooded slopes, or the banks of a stream, or a rocky hillside turned into an enchanting garden. If they are truly enchanting, it will be found that they dominate their surroundings, including the house (unless the garden is far enough away from the house not to count). Their charm will be found to lie in their suitability to their site and not in blindly following the conventions of informal gardening.

No definite style of garden from the past answers all the needs of today's small garden. Many gardens from the past help us to understand the underlying principles of building gardens for maximum enjoyment. There were the smart town gardens of Pompeii; the courtyard gardens of Spain; the walled flower gardens of Queen Elizabeth and Henry VIII. They all contributed to our knowledge of scale and livability as applied to the areas surrounding the house. This is a new era in garden making, because while many things have entered our life to make the problem complex, our ideas and requirements tend toward simplicity of solution.

Changes in garden design during the last few decades have been enormous. Unless you have had the opportunity to see the best new houses of recent years, you can hardly realize how completely and basically the garden has changed.

Even the term "garden" has changed its meaning. A garden used to have a horticultural meaning—a place where plants were grown to be displayed for mass effects or to be examined individually. It was a place to walk through, to sit in briefly while you contemplated the wonders of nature before you returned to the civilized safety of the indoors. It was generally designed to provide a long vista from some dramatic spot within the house, such as the entry hall, the front steps, or a bay window. It was a place to be looked at rather than a place to be lived in.

The new kind of garden is still supposed to be looked at. But that is no longer its only function. It is designed primarily for living, as an adjunct to the functions of the house. How well it provides for the many types of living that can be carried on outdoors is the new standard by which we judge a garden.

This change in our ideas of what a garden is supposed to do for us was brought about by the force of several circumstances: the shrinking of the size of our houses due to high building costs, the disappearance of gardeners, the coming of power tools, and the increased use of glass. As the house grew smaller, many functions that used to go on inside the house were forced into less expensive space. Smaller rooms set up the need for bigger windows and whole walls of glass—to dissipate the feeling of claustrophobia. So presently it became inevitable that the garden should attach itself to the house, not only in use but structurally and visually. The garden had to go to work for us, solving our living problems while it also pleased our eyes and our emotional and psychological needs.

So a new trend was born—out of human necessities. No arbitrary whims or designer's caprices created this new kind of garden. It evolved naturally and inevitably from people's requirements. And out of the solutions to these requirements has come a whole new visual aesthetic, contributed to by many landscape designers in many parts of the country. Though this new kind of garden design was born out of the problems of new houses, it has lately been applied to the old as well. For it helps us get more usefulness from our property and gives a new usefulness to old houses.

Peace and ease are the dominant characteristics of the new garden—peace and beauty for the eye and ease of maintenance for the owner. Fewer and simpler lines are being used in the garden, and fewer and simpler materials. All is calculated to give complete restfulness to the eye. If the eye sees too many things, it is confused and the sense of peace is obliterated.

Simplification of lines does not mean eliminating outdoor structure. The closer house and garden are, in use and appearance, the more they begin to interlock visually. More and more the lines and materials of the house are carried outdoors and into the landscape. And more and more the materials of the garden structure penetrate into the house, recalling the outside design and subtly merging indoors and outdoors. The paving of the terrace is penetrating into the house, making the floors more utilitarian in such heavy-duty spots as hallways, stairways, and heavy traffic areas.

Since the garden is being designed more and more to be seen from several parts of the house, the plan of it cannot be rigid and set, with a beginning and an end. The lines of the modern garden must be moving and flowing, so that it is pleasing when seen from all directions, both inside and out.

The eye can be easily fooled. Things can be made to seem longer or wider than they really are. This is a great aid, for we can make a small lot seem bigger, and so create spaciousness, without increasing garden maintenance and real estate taxes. Thus a moving, changing line that creates an asymmetric plan not only pleases the eye but creates a new dimension for the house.

To succeed in making a logical and intelligent plan which will produce the maximum in terms of use and beauty, one must have simplicity of layout, integrity in the use of plant and structural materials, and a sure sense of proportion and pleasing form. Whether your design is "formal" or "informal", curved or straight, symmetrical or free, or a combination of all, the important thing is that you end up with a functional plan and an artistic composition. It must have good proportion and proper scale and plants that have been chosen wisely and cared for affectionately.

Rhythm and movement are essential. You expect them in the pictures you hang on your wall, in the music you listen to, in the poetry you read. In the garden it's the wind in the foliage and the dog running across the lawn. It's the line of the terrace and the repetition of richly textured foliage. The eye is a restless organ.

Symmetry can have motion. It's unimaginative formality that can become static. The eye prefers to move around a garden on lines that are provocative, never lose their interest, never end in dead corners, occasionally provide excitement or surprise, and always leave you interested and contented.

Someone may say, "I don't want it formal, laid out on an axis." The truth is your garden is never without at least one axis and probably has two or three. All compositions, however free, are built around them. The great designers of natural gardens may seem to have thrown away their T squares, but the axis is just as strong as in the mirror pool of the Taj Mahal. It's just less obvious.

The axis becomes visual rather than mechanical and needn't be at right angles to the eye. The eye is tolerant. It may be influenced by a view, nudged by a tree, encouraged by a meadow, or seduced by a brook. Don't fret if your garden is never quite perfect. Absolute perfection, like complete consistency, can be dull.

Garden Details

What are the important details, and what structural materials are available to enrich the design of a garden? Even with a good plan the success of the garden will depend upon:

The intelligent placing, spacing, and interrelationship of the various elements;

Understanding the possibilities and limits of structural and plant materials;

Discreetly evaluating the weakness and strength of various colors and textures;

Choosing materials which are sympathetic with the site, with each other, and with the people who are to see and use them.

Today's garden, with its avowed purpose of providing convenient pleasures and pleasant conveniences, will include some or all of the following:

Fences and walls: for protection and privacy

Retaining walls: when the bulldozer leaves the property looking as if it had been hit by a blockbuster

Steps: for lots too steep for ramps; or for flat lots where differences in elevation are artificially created to add interest

Paving: concrete, brick, gravel, etc. for terraces, walks, and service areas, to avoid tracking mud and to reduce maintenance

Trees: for shade and shelter

Plants: for color, texture, form and mass

Water: in pools for swimming, dipping, wading, fish, and lilies

Sculpture: suited to an outdoor setting

Playing space for children: where they will be safe, contented, and easily watched

Built-in seating: to save moving too much furniture too often

Storage walls: to take the overflow

Raised flower and vegetable beds: for neatness and convenience

Mowing strips: to define lawn and planting areas and to simplify grass cutting

Service yard and garden work area: for incinerators, potting bench, mulch bin, tools, ad infinitum

Photograph by Maynard L. Parker

". . . as most of the comforts and all
the elegancies and refinements of life
consist in attention to numerous small
matters which are, in themselves,
insignificant, but which together
compose a beautiful and agreeable
whole, so the expression and character
of a garden will be cultivated and
tasteful or otherwise according as its
minor features are well arranged and
well executed."

KEMP, *Landscape Gardening*, 1850

Forced Perspective, the Illusion of Space

Make-believe is always appealing, and to the designer, who is often faced with a small garden wishing it were twice as large, it's a fine trick of the trade. Various means of creating an illusion of space have been used, depending upon the century and the country in which the gardens were built.

The French call their solution "trompe l'oeil," and during the seventeenth and eighteenth centuries they developed this technique in gardens by using and combining trelliswork, mirrors, painted murals, foreshortened paths, and vistas. Under their capable hands, a flat wall enclosing an oppressive space became an invitation to leave the house and enjoy the out-of-doors. Its promise was difficult to resist. John Evelyn, in 1642, describes a well-painted perspective as "a very agreeable deceit," and Humphry Repton, writing in 1795, says, "Nor is the imagination so fastidious as to take offense at any well supported deception, even after the want of reality is discovered." Such false perspectives can compensate for the restrictions of small city gardens, wherever they are.

Illustrated here is an entryway from which the only view was the depressing-looking blank wall of the neighboring house. By using trompe l'oeil lattice on the wall, the house appears to have receded and the garden space has visually increased.

Photographs by Maynard L. Parker

Steps in Design

When a broad flight of steps can also retain a change in grade, the question of whether it should be curved or straight may come up.

There is no rule to determine this other than the overall garden design. It's a matter of creating contrast in the composition. A curve seems more so if it has contrast to the strength of a straight line. The interplay of curving and linear forms adds zest to the pattern. It is the prerogative of the designer to decide where the emphasis should be placed.

Once the question of design is settled, there are practical precedents as to use of materials. Brick or stone, being modular, is easy for building curved flights. A straight run may be of brick, stone, concrete, or wood. The choice again reverts back to the need for using materials harmonious with each other, with the architecture, and with the mood of the garden.

Steps can be much more than a connection between two levels. They can have strength and crispness of line. They can steady the composition, point the direction, and ornament the scene.

They may be used to express the mood and tempo of the garden. They can put you in a leisurely mood, make you hurry, or arouse your curiosity.

Use them with care and forethought.

Curves in Step Design

The steps in these illustrations are of red brick, held together with white mortar. The wall, in both cases, has been whitewashed to accent further the graceful curves and to provide additional contrast in color.

Photograph by John Robinson

A Line Can Lead Your Eye Around a Corner

By a curve or an angle or any strong combination of lines in plants and structural materials, the designer may lead the eye in any direction he chooses. Here the existing court was well related to the living and dining rooms but not to the garden, much of which was hidden around the corner of the house.

With the paving extended and the steps turned at a 45° angle, the terrace and garden flow together. The eye is lazy and easily led.

Photograph by Rondal Partridge

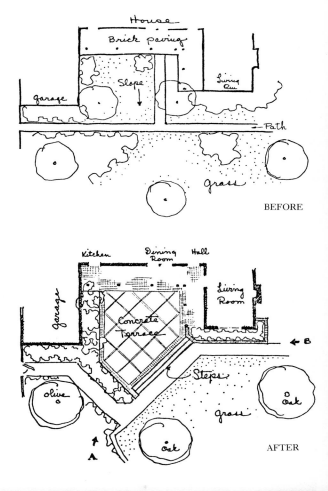

Create a Calm Composition

Gardens can create an emotion; a cluttered, random, untended garden can arouse feelings of dislike and discomfort, while a garden in harmony with itself and its surroundings can give the viewer an immediate feeling of serenity and peace.

Planting

Yesterday's houses were high off the ground, needing a buffer of lilacs to relate them to the garden. Today they are low and friendly, sitting at ground level. The foundation has disappeared, but the habit of planting to hide it still remains.

Too much enthusiasm in planting at the base of a house can do a garden in quicker than anything else. It is a shame to veil any house in shrubbery when the house itself is well designed. To heavily fringe such a house with foundation planting is to deny its architectural entity and to negate the strength it gives to the garden composition. The relationship between the house and garden is maintained and emphasized by light, air, and visual space flowing freely from one to the other.

Restraint in planting and enthusiasm in its maintenance is the alternative. This approach may result in using an occasional plant to soften the house outline but will still permit the outline to be positively stated by paving all along its base. With most of the planting moved further out into the garden, it can also be enjoyed from inside the house, and the home will make its full contribution to the garden composition. Instead of watching your house gradually disappear in a morass of various foliages, fighting for light and air in front and gathering leaves and cobwebs in the rear, think about using low evergreens that will not get out of hand. Perhaps all you really need is a vine and an occasional plant. Paving and grass can now approach the house without a buffer of shrubbery.

A tree, placed to frame the house or cast its shadow on it, does more softening than a forest of shrubs.

Heavy planting can be pushed to the boundaries, allowing the house and garden to become better acquainted.

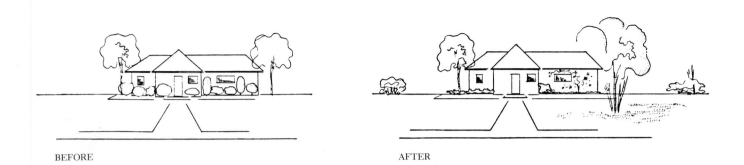

BEFORE   AFTER

Avoid Foundation Planting

The garden shown here gave the house a smothered feeling. Rooms became dark too early in the day, and visitors had to grope around the shrubbery to reach the front door.

With its unsightly excess padding of overgrown bushes and trees sheared away, this charming house appears to be years younger than before.

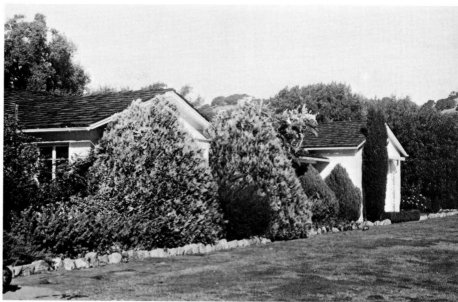

Maintenance Influences Both
Design and Materials

People want their gardens to provide many pleasures, conveniences, and comforts; none but dyed-in-the-wool gardeners want them to be any work.

There is, of course, no such thing as a 100 percent maintenance-free garden, and if there were you would soon tire of it, for it would cease to be a garden. Most people mean they want the space so organized that they may know the delights of gardening in what little time they have; that they will not become a slave to a scheme that never looks its best no matter how much time they labor at it.

Photograph by Rondal Partridge

Large areas should be under permanent control (lawns, ground covers, paving). Most of the planting should be in permanent and slower-growing materials. Frayed edges and unmanageable corners should be worked over.

What is a good substitute for lawn? There is none—nothing that has its bright color in contrast to other garden greens or its texture or tactile quality. The ground covers—lippia, dichondra, ivy, pachysandra, etc.—all have their place, require little care under proper conditions, and can be used to reduce the amount of lawn. Think twice, however, because once you are behind the lawn mower you might as well cut a little more, and for year-round care few materials give you so much for so little.

". . . and with turfes new Fresh turved, whereof the grene gras So smal, so thick, so short, so fresh of hew That most like unto green wool wot I it was."
CHAUCER, *The Flower and the Leafe*, 1400

Photograph by Maynard L. Parker

Paving Can Reduce Maintenance

There's no doubt that more garden space can be covered with hard-surfaced materials and the result be both aesthetic and practical.

The average driveway is too narrow, the parking space too cramped, the terraces too small, and the paths too mean in dimension; there are places in deep shade where nothing will grow and little-used corners which can be paved and be the better for it, thus decreasing the amount of maintained area.

Photograph by Maynard L. Parke

This garden is calm, restful, and serene, inviting contemplation. Why? Because maintenance is minimal. Hard-packed gravel was rolled for paving, and the plants are few in number but treated as friends. Any battle between a gardener and consuming foliage is not evident. Designed for a hot, dry climate, the scheme has vigor yet repose; it has a sense of belonging in nature, yet a feeling that man is at home in his surroundings.

This close relationship to natural environment is the height of true formalism; you will find it in well-tended New England woodlands, in the azalea gardens of the South, in the rocky sand gardens of Arizona, and especially in the eloquent simplicity of Japanese gardens.

Photograph by Maynard L. Parker

Mowing Strips

Narrow bands of hard paving, level with and at the edges of a lawn, provide a track for one wheel of the mower, minimize hand trimming, and keep the grass shape intact and free from encroaching plants.

They provide a decorative, permanent border and strengthen the garden pattern where a crisp, neat line is desired.

Photograph by Maynard L. Parker

The Raised Bed

We all know the undeniable charm of strolling down a garden path brilliant with annuals and winding through an informal garden filled with flowery surprises and delights. Gardens like this exist, and true gardeners are eager and willing to spend the time and care to maintain the casual and cluttered perfection this type of garden offers through the seasons.

Most of us, however, need a garden area which is always neat and ordered with a minimum of work. Sacrificed are the heady delights of dividing perennials in the fall, mulching the hibiscus for the winter, and the thousand and one fascinating chores that need doing through the year. The raised bed has advantages—it reduces upkeep, is easier to keep neat and trim, improves plant culture through better soil drainage, keeps dogs and children out of flower or vegetable areas, and provides a ledge on which to sit.

The garden shown here has neat edges, crisp forms, and permanent materials. There are raised beds for cut flowers, roses, and flowering trees. The emphasis is on a garden which will look well all through the year. Careful planning makes it enjoyable with a minimum amount of upkeep.

Double Walls Were the Solution for This Garden

A garden can be easier to look at, as well as to maintain, if certain planting areas are raised above the main grade. If you have a high retaining wall or fence and want to reduce its visual impact, a raised bed at the base will perform miracles. Your eye will subtract the lower level from the overall vertical height and negate the problem.

A flat lot may need this subtlety as well as a hillside, which may demand it. If pulling a weed or plucking a flower is a chore at ground level, a raised bed can halve the strain and double the pleasure.

Photograph by Michael Laurie

Curbs Keep a Garden Neat

They may be low and simply define a planting space, or they may be high and broad and comfortable to sit on. They may be used in a flower or vegetable garden to create raised beds at a convenient working height.

The greatest value of curbs around planting beds is their ability to contain a design which might otherwise be obliterated by time and planting. The pattern will be retained even if the beds are unplanted. If a softer effect is desired, use low hedges or borders.

Paris

Photograph by Maynard L. Parker

The rose garden is set on a brick platform 6 inches high, and the rose beds are raised another 6 inches in redwood curbs.

Here, curbs provide crispness and shadow and keep the garden looking neat and well tended.

In this garden they are of wood, but they could be built of brick, stone, or any other desirable material.

Raising this part of the garden has resulted in additional interest on an otherwise flat lot; it was done primarily to provide 12 inches of topsoil for the roses in an area of heavy soil and poor drainage.

Privacy from the Street

The owners of this house wanted privacy
from the street and yet enable their guests
to arrive pleasantly and park easily.

The photograph illustrates the use of a
double hedge along a sidewalk, a device to
provide elbow room, recommended when a
sense of space is required instead of the
abruptness of a hedge rising directly from the
edge of the walk.

The low planting next to the sidewalk, as
shown, covers the thin places that often
occur at the base of a tall hedge. In this case,
the high hedge is privet and the low is
pittosporum. Both are kept carefully clipped
to assure a well-tailored look. The trees cut
off the sight line from the house across the
street.

Screen a Seasonal Garden

Vegetable and cutting gardens are great assets to the garden, but it is impossible to keep them at the prime of visual perfection throughout the year. Vegetables and flowers have seasons and can look ragged as they begin to fade into the long, dormant winter. The last rose of summer deserves credit for perseverance but may not add much to the view from the terrace.

The objective of this design was to screen the beds from the terrace yet not put them in a high-walled compound of their own. A series of baffled walls lets them be part of the garden yet not constantly in view.

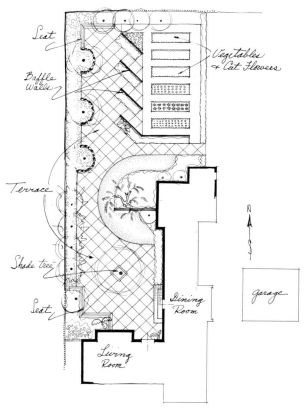

Pleasant Deceit

A problem facing many city dwellers with a small but precious space in the rear garden is the existence of a neighbor's garage on the property line.

To screen it with plants takes invaluable footage from an already restricted space. To plant trees may create shade where the owners want sun.

On the theory that the neighbor never sees it anyway—and granting that he's cooperative—here is a solution which makes it seem really all yours.

Admittedly, the door is pure whimsy, since it goes nowhere—but it might and is thus an invitation to come onto its terrace.

New vertical siding, a few moldings, and an old door from the wreckers plus a brick terrace and appropriate plantings have created the illusion of space, comfort, and welcome.

BEFORE: A neighbor's unsightly garage.

AFTER: Architecturally interesting.

Children's Needs Affect Design

Children love to go around and around, whether it's on a merry-go-round or in their own backyard. Perhaps it has something to do with a feeling of speed, or the excitement of the race and the chase, or just returning again and again to the familiar. One thing is certain: a circular route in the garden can provide more amusement hours for small children than any number of swings or slides.

This fact can influence the design of a garden, particularly a small one with more demands on each square foot of space than it can possibly satisfy. It has to be attractive all year, useful for entertaining, easily maintained, and adaptable to the children so they will be content to play at home a good part of the time.

The circular grass area pictured here is simple but highly satisfactory to the whole family. It is defined by a concrete border, which serves as a mowing band for easier care and a circular route for tricycles, wagons, and skates.

Garden Work Areas and Service Yards

Every garden should have a place to pot a plant, to store the fertilizers, to hang up the tools, and to build a compost pit. It may vary in size from a workbench and closet to an efficient gardening center. Ready-made greenhouses, cold frames, lath houses, and storage walls may be combined to make any desired arrangement.

A service yard can include many things, but storage for gardening equipment and tools and the overflow from the house seem to be what people need most.

A down-to-earth gardener is an experimenter, a putterer, and a collector. He can spend countless happy hours making cuttings, trying out new sprays, and speculating on the results of a new soil mix.

These and all other activities of a garden work area can be pursued more fruitfully in a space that is conveniently planned. A workbench wide enough to hold flats, accessible storage for tools and miscellany, and potting soil close at hand are important considerations. Sun, shade, and surfaces are also needed.

Service areas are as important to the functioning of a garden as the kitchen is to the house and should always be included in the overall planning.

Photograph by Maynard L. Parker

Garden Architecture

Entrances

The Arrival—Welcome!

T he psychology of arrival is more important than one thinks.
  If it is not obvious where to park, if there is no room to park when you get there, if you stumble into the back door looking for the front entrance, or if the entrance is badly lighted, your guests have been subjected to a series of annoyances which will linger long in their subconscious.

No matter how warm your hearth or how beautiful your view, the overall effect will be dimmed by these first irritations. Nothing justifies making an obstacle course out of the trip from the car to the front door.

It will require the finest food and the most comfortable chair to make up for being obliged to walk through mud, or having your hat knocked off by overhanging trees and your stockings ripped on the pyracantha.

The size of walks, arrival areas, and platforms must be adjusted to the scale of the building. But in all cases, there should be enough room for a group of people to wait for the bell to be answered or to linger over good-byes. Your guest should always feel that the act of arriving has been effortless, and leaving, equally so.

"There is commonly a great propensity to make the sweeps of gravel at an entrance door for carriages to turn in a good deal too large for the accommodation of careless coachmen . . . The smaller the space that can possibly be turned in the better it will look."
KEMP, *Landscape Gardening,* 1850

Residence of John Donnelly,
San Mateo, California

The Importance of the Entrance Cannot Be Overemphasized

In making the entrance a place of welcome, simplicity and harmony are the most important ingredients. To emphasize an obvious but strangely overlooked fact: the entrance should be designed to show where your front door is. The lines of the paths and planting may be used to increase the importance of the entrance and make it a pleasure to arrive.

The small house appears larger and assumes dignity and importance when it is saved from the obscurity of heavy planting. A simple planting scheme will not compete with the house for attention.

Paving, carried to the house foundation, reaffirms the fact that the house has stability and intends to remain in the community.

Properly placed trees near an entrance add shade and interest, help screen the window from the street, and tend to visually set the house further back on the lot. The expanse of paving here is relieved by a pocket for a tree and low planting. Note the softening effect of the tree's shadow on concrete.

Photograph by Philip Fein

Photograph by Carolyn Caddes

Give your guests plenty of elbowroom outside the front door or garden gate, so they may feel they have arrived before they ring the bell. Let them enjoy the planting, the architecture, the paving patterns in an area scaled to their anticipation of the hospitality just over the threshold.

A few extra square feet of space outside the front door lends a graciousness to the whole experience of being a guest.

Too often the drive, the walk, and the entry platform are of three different materials. The scheme in this quiet and elegant entrance to a suburban house is simplified by using one material only. Wisteria and golden honey locust trees add color.

A Town House Entrance

When you step off the sidewalk and enter your home grounds, you should have the feeling that it's your own private world. Why be saddled with inadequate planting? Why be chagrined because your neighbor's drive flanks your walk? Why be annoyed by the lack of privacy in your front yard?

There are solutions to these problems. A little expense and a great deal of planning are necessary, to be sure, but are worthwhile in the long run.

The town house shown here now has a quiet, secluded entrance garden. The formal facade has been recognized and accented by moving the entrance to the center. The wall alleviates the confusion once created by the juxtaposition of the house next door. The over age yew trees have been retired (to a country lane, we hope) and replaced here with roundheaded Victoria box (*Pittosporum undulatum*). Most of all, the composition has assumed the quiet dignity befitting a town house.

BEFORE: A hodgepodge frontage

AFTER: Seclusion and unity are gained by walling in the forecourt. The facade of the house now joins an inviting entrance walk.

An Entrance Garden

An enclosed court-garden makes a delightful entrance. For this house in Santa Barbara, California, the garden gates open to welcome one into an easily maintained entrance garden consisting of a three-level paved terrace, existing boulders, and a few plants—all placed to take advantage of the picturesquely beautiful oak trees, a grove of which is one of the main features of the site.

The covered walkway leads directly to the front door, and at night the trees are lighted from below by floodlights.

Photograph by Maynard L. Parker

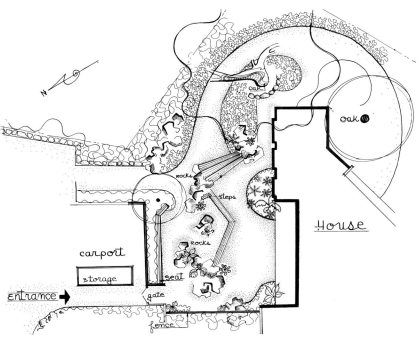

Photographs by Maynard L. Parker

Photograph by Ernest Braun

Your Entrance Should Say "Welcome," and the Steps Should be an Invitation.

In this garden the "stoop" and its steps have been moved 30 feet out to the driveway to provide a continuous red carpet to the front door.

Steps Are For People

The primary function of steps is to get from one level to another. However, their possibilities as an important factor in design have been apparent throughout all the ages of building.

Their shape, extent, and material may be influenced by the absolute scale of the overall composition, but their final allegiance is to the people who use them; and in detail they must never fail to relate to the scale of the human figure.

Designers use steps in their compositions to produce emotion, to be a visual and actual welcome into their designs, to form strong and dynamic horizontal lines across their buildings. Their scale, shape, direction, material, and decoration are subject to infinite variety, limited only by the designer's imagination.

While few of us want, or can have, our steps done in the grand manner, we can learn a great deal by studying early examples. Their scale, flow of line, and dramatic quality have never been equaled.

Villa d'Este, Tivoli.

Photograph by Thomas Church

Steps Are for Steep Sites

A long flight of steps on a steep site can be more important than you intend. Too much masonry, too many retaining walls and landings can overpower all other elements in the garden.

The steps above overcame a difference in elevation of 14 feet, yet they remain calm as they wind down around the tree. With the stone wall only along one side, they descend the hill quietly. The risers are 7 inches, the treads 12 inches.

Steps Are an Invitation

Wide, comfortable, properly designed and located, steps are one of the main devices by which the observer may be enticed into the garden.

They should be so placed that they may be used without constantly crossing conversation groups or quiet garden areas.

The curved terrace line, shown below, flows to wide steps that invite you to explore the upper level.

The size of a flight of steps will be influenced by its use as well as by the distance between the levels and their importance to the whole design.

Two people need 5 feet in which to walk comfortably down a flight of steps together.

Steps can be narrow and increase the visual separation of two levels, or they can be broad and make two separate areas appear to be one.

The Riser-and-Tread Relationship

This will make or break your steps. Don't think you're making it easier by making them lower. If you hear that 6-inch risers and 14-inch treads make a comfortable garden step (correct), don't try to make it still easier by reducing the riser to 4 inches unless you change the tread width as well.

A rule to respect is: Twice the riser plus the tread equals 26 inches. So if you want a 4-inch riser, you need an 18-inch tread. All steps should have ⅛- to ¼-inch pitch (included in the riser dimension) to shed water.

If, to make the grade, you have to use an 8-inch riser, use a 10-inch tread (the proportions of the old cellar step.) At a recent cotillion, thirteen out of sixteen debutantes tripped into the arms of their escorts as they descended the stairs. It was found that the steps had 5-inch risers and 12-inch treads (5 inches + 5 inches + 12 inches = 22 inches). They had been made low to make it easy for the girls to glide down gracefully. If the risers had been 5 inches and the treads 16 inches, the girls could have floated down as if on a cloud.

Steps to Separate

Retaining walls tend to separate areas in a garden, but sometimes the designer wants to minimize existing differences between levels. Often he prefers the areas to flow together as an expanse, both for visual effect and for ease of use. Broad steps used as a retaining element instead of a vertical wall can solve the problem. With steps, there is no reason for a railing to separate the areas further. There is no need to worry about extra chairs for party seating.

The most important consideration is the riser-tread relationship. Only cellar steps can have steep and stingy dimensions; a broad flight, in particular, must have gracious proportions.

Rome can get away with the Spanish Steps, but the domestic-scaled garden can't cope with broad flights of more than half a dozen steps. They are an exceedingly strong design element, but properly related to the overall scheme, their dominance adds interest and unity to the garden.

Seats

Gardens Are Made to Sit In

There's nothing more inviting than large, comfortable furniture on a large, comfortable terrace.

But there's a limit to storage space and a limit to one's patience when too many chairs have to be moved in out of the rain. Permanently built seats can accommodate large groups in a garden with a minimum amount of movable furniture. Visually the seats become part of the overall design, cutting sharp shadows and creating strong patterns.

Although the most comfortable width is 18 inches, seats may be as wide as 30 inches, so people can sit on either side or use them as buffet or cocktail tables.

They may be open underneath where a feeling of lightness is desired or when the line of vision should not be stopped, and especially when paving or grass continue beyond the seat.

They may be free-standing or retain a tree, a house wall, or a slope.

A narrow retaining wall may become a useful garden feature by the addition of a cap wide enough to sit on, and besides, the added width is pleasanter to look at.

The Terrace

The Terrace May Be Flowing or Formal in Outline

Today's terrace is no longer thought of as a small rectangle directly off the living room; it may go around the house or wander over a large portion of the property.

It may reach out some distance and at seemingly odd and unpredictable angles, seeking a tree for shade, securing a vantage point for a view, or avoiding rough topography.

It can be generous in extent or intimate in feeling; not so big that it looks like a corporation yard nor so small that one is pushed into the flower beds. It can encompass grass plots, flower beds, potted plants, arbors, sun platforms, windscreens, sand for the children, and a drinking fountain for the dog.

It should have comfortable furniture with convenient storage and easy access to the living room and kitchen. The terrace should do all these things, as well as put some people in the sun, some in the shade, and others out of a draft.

The problems of design, orientation, and materials vary enormously in different parts of the country. In some sections the garden and terrace may be 90 percent paved and be a logical solution. In others, the lawn may be the terrace.

The problem may be protection from wind in San Francisco or reaching out for a breeze in St. Louis. The terrace may be designed largely for use at night in Texas or require screening in the mosquito belt. It may need shade most of the time or sun most of the time (the terrace large enough for both is ideal).

"Some fine pavement about it, doeth well."
FRANCIS BACON, *Of Gardens*, 1625

This spacious brick terrace outside the living room is a good example of the indoor-outdoor living of our time. It is a transition from the formality of the house to the natural surroundings; a transition so subtle that one is scarcely aware of the change.

The overhang and tree provide shade in the heat of summer.

Photograph by Philip Fein

Photograph by Maynard L. Parker

This scheme borrows line and simplicity of layout from the French formal gardens but is reduced in size to fit modern living.

Planned as a green garden, it is surrounded by a yew hedge and hawthorns. Small boxwood parterres with bright colors are in the center of the sunken garden.

The terrace is sunk below the lawn in order to avoid branches of the oak tree. It is shaded when the house terrace is in full sun and provides interest on an otherwise flat lot.

The brick retaining wall doubles as a seat.

Our terraces today must be in scale with what we expect them to do for us.

The terrace illustrated is immediately in front of the main conservatory at Longwood, Pennsylvania, and is scaled in proportion to the surrounding gardens. The large area, with its fish-scale-pattern floor design, connects the conservatory with the uninterrupted view of the fountain gardens to be seen in the distance.

otograph by courtesy of Longwood Gardens, Pennsylvania

This brick terrace was designed to curve to
one side of the house axis. From here, the
owners have an unobstructed view of the
distant hills. The lawn inset provides a
verdant island in the patterned terrace
surface. Potted plants mark the terrace
perimeter.

Boldness in Design

Timidity in garden design is never more clearly demonstrated than when you reach the edge of a precipice. Stopping there shatters the proportions of the open spaces, leaves the house looking as though it is about to tip over the brink, and denies you the pleasure of ever being far enough removed from your house to be able to look back and admire it.

The addition of this semicircular terrace denies any timid compromise with the slope. It seems to be reaching out for an oak tree growing in the canyon and provides a serene, integrated composition with the house.

Photograph by Maynard L. Parker

"If you are discreet, you will realize that one terrace, well kept up, is much more valuable than several left in disrepair."

ALBERT MAUMONE, *The Garden*, Paris, 1932

"It ought to lie to the best Parts of the House, or to those of the Master's Commonest Use, so as to be but like one of those Rooms out of which you step into another."

SIR WILLIAM TEMPLE, *Of Gardening*, 1685

Photographs by Maynard L. Parker

Put a Small Terrace Where You'll Use It

There may be special-purpose terraces other than the main one.

Small, quiet places to read the morning paper and enjoy the second cup of coffee, sunbathe, or shell the peas may be outside any door or deep in the garden. Their location is a matter of convenience.

If the terrace is for lunching, it should be easily reached from the kitchen (unless it's for picnics and hiking to it is considered an excursion).

If it's for an afternoon siesta, it should be relatively quiet, with trees strategically placed for swinging a hammock.

If it's for sunbathing, it should be private and sheltered from the wind.

You must look for conditions that suit the special purpose of the terrace—a point from which there is a view hidden from the house or where the sun shines at a certain hour; a spot where there's an afternoon breeze in the summer or protection from the wind in the fall; or an area that makes a sun pocket in the snow.

Move in and live with your property before you make all the decisions.

"Places are not to be laid out with a view to their appearance in a picture, but to their uses, and the enjoyment of them in real life; and their conformity to those purposes is that which constitutes their beauty . . ."
RT. HON. WILLIAM WINDHAM,
in a letter to Humphry Repton, 1794

A Terrace May Be Away from the House

When possible, a part of the terrace should be far enough away so that the view back to the house is pleasant. The areas around it compose best only from a certain distance. If your terrace is small and you sit with your back to your own house, you may look only at your neighbor's.

If your neighbor's house is better looking than yours, don't read any farther.

Try walking around your house. In some places you will walk fast, but sooner or later you will reach a spot where you feel in repose. It may be the lines of the house or the position of trees, or you may never know why; but it could be the place for your terrace.

Decks

The wooden balconies of eighteenth-century European design were forerunners, and the spacious front porches and verandas of English and American architecture during the Victorian era were ancestors. But porches have become detached from houses and wander freely around the property—sometimes jutting out over it, providing the illusion of level spaciousness on a sloping hillside lot. These wandering porches, which, in one form or another, have been with us for a long time, are now what we call decks.

As the deck becomes more and more important to us for both aesthetic and practical reasons, we are more and more aware of its varied uses; the dominant line of a fill may be broken and consequently softened, the shade of a tree may be welcomed in a sitting area, the last hour of sun may be relished; the house may be viewed from a certain distance so that it is seen in the full round instead of in profile.

For the home owner on a budget—and name one who isn't—a deck can serve as the ideal compromise, using natural materials in an outdoor setting but retaining the low-maintenance attractions of a practical space paved in concrete.

The creation of flat terraces around trees already growing on slopes is inexcusable. When the normal breathing and drainage are disturbed, trees become sickly and die, and sooner or later the sitting area is no longer under an inviting canopy of green. Drainage and aeration may prevent such a calamity, but why take a chance when decks offer a safe alternative?

Decks are at home among the tree trunks, and people are happy when they are among the trees. As with the garden shown here, a deck made it possible to enjoy a close relationship with the native oaks at the floor level of the house. And, most important, the lives of the trees are not endangered.

Photograph by Maynard L. Parker

Photograph by Rondal Partridge

Bridging from the house terrace, this redwood deck floats into the treetops, 20 feet above the ground and 40 feet into the foliage, shade, and shadow. There is a sense of levitation here that could only be duplicated by a space platform.

Here is a place for quiet contemplation, bird-watching, unhurried reading, and unparalleled views of the ferns and azaleas below.

Civilization has moved us out of trees and into houses, yet the magic of life in the treetops persists. As children we find fascination in tree houses. As adults, we can recapture the mood by building decks high among the tree branches. So doing, we learn the fact that trees mean much more to us when we are close to them. The sky seems bluer when viewed through foliage, and a vista has depth and perspective when framed by tree branches.

On the deck illustrated here, the white band between the redwood and the pebble covering on the terrace is the top of the concrete retaining wall built along the original slope from which the deck takes off into space. A 2-foot seat is placed at the edge of the deck.

Photograph by Maynard L. Parker

Fences

Today's economic pressures dictate that houses in our subdivisions be built only a few feet apart; you decide you must put up a fence, but what kind? The house material, other fences in the neighborhood, your personal likes and dislikes, and your budget will all influence your choice.

Wire and wood fences are least expensive and easiest to build. Wood lends itself to the greatest variety of patterns, combinations, and colors. The amateur carpenter–owner can install a good-looking fence himself on weekends.

Realize that although the fence can be an important asset to the garden, it shouldn't dominate its surroundings. Too elaborate a combination of squares, triangles, or free forms or too many bright colors may overpower not only the garden but the Matisse in the living room.

There's no right or wrong side to a fence any more. The back side of a wood fence has disappeared; the post and frame, which used to be turned away or covered with siding, has become a potential design factor.

A fence can be kept plain or made exciting, depending on the mood of the garden. It can be used to create definite patterns and strong shadows. It can be dark, to make it recede, or light, to bring it forward. It can be solid, for complete privacy, partially open or louvered to appear light and airy, or mostly open to suggest a boundary without being a barrier. It can be zigzagged to become part of the general garden design.

Photograph by John Robinson ▽

△ Photograph by John Robinson
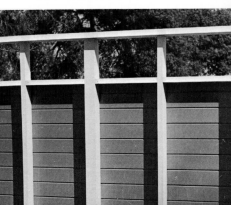

An Oasis from a Shunned Site

BEFORE: The unshaded, bright, unattractive, and uncared-for part of this garden seemed to have little prospect. But it did have some positive aspects. It was protected from the wind and directly related to the living room of the house. It seemed the ideal place for a terrace and, in the climate of California, a swimming pool.

AFTER: What a difference planning can accomplish!

A wood deck was built at floor level to cut down the glare, and a pavilion provided shade and forced the outsize chimney into proper scale. The pool is integrated with the terrace, which juts into it and defines a wading area yet leaves plenty of room for swimming.

Surrounded by grass and flowering trees, this once-shunned backyard has now become an oasis used all year round.

© Photograph by Morley Baer

A Focus at the End of the Terrace

This summerhouse, with an Oriental flavor, marks the top of a terraced flower garden. Leading up the hillside to it, the wood retaining walls are built at angles bending toward you rather than perpendicular to the central path. This subtle detail in construction opens up the flower beds to a wider angle and gives an illusion of a larger area.

It is a symmetrical layout with a balanced planting of flowering cherry trees and a wide assortment of spring-blooming bulbs, annuals, and perennials.

Twin Gazebos in a Formal Garden

These latticed gazebos punctuate the symmetrical elegance of this garden. They provide entertainment areas and are decorative year-round features when viewed from the house.

Silhouetted against the hill, the two tall pavilions dominate the terraced garden.

Photograph by Maynard L. Parker

This open-structure teahouse provides an
attractive shelter for outdoor meals and is a
focal point of the garden.

Architecturally Sound

An old lath house sat in the middle of this proposed pool and garden space.

You couldn't see through it or around it, yet, with its curved roof and sound structure, it survived to become the pool lanai and garden entertainment area.

With the roof retained and the sides removed, it is a light, airy structure around which the whole scheme revolves.

Behind the brick wall is a small summer kitchen, shower, and dressing room.

Photograph by Rondal Partridge

BEFORE: A dingy white elephant, a covered bridge to nowhere.

Photograph by Rondal Partridge

A Pergola for Interest on a Flat Site

The pergola from southern Italy has a
humble origin, being nothing more than a
succession of rustic poles used to support
grapevines. Developed from this is the
heavy-timbered pergola, with a decorative
elevated roof in its rear corner, illustrated.
Backed by a high evergreen hedge, it reaches
out as an architectural frame to support the
Wisteria floribunda and to give shade in an
otherwise unsheltered sitting area.

In this garden wisteria vines have also been
trained as trees, planted in beds with curbs
sufficiently heavy to be in scale with the
trunks as they mature and in scale with the
nearby pergola.

Photograph by courtesy of Longwood Gardens, Pennsylvania

Photograph by Bruce Harlow

The Shelter by the Pool

Whatever the structure by the pool is called—"cabana," "pool house," "lanai," or "garden room"—it serves many purposes. It can provide dressing rooms, space for filter and heating equipment, a storage area for garden furniture and barbecue tools, and a summer kitchen for outdoor entertaining.

Illustrated is a pool house transformed from a former outbuilding whose stone structure once supported a water tank. The tank was removed and a second floor added, topped by a red-cedar-shingle mansard roof; the dormer windows are replicas of those on the main house. The structure is electrically heated and provides a charming guest room.

Photograph by Carolyn Caddes

Photograph by Michael Laurie

5

The Palette

Rich in tradition and colorful in content, the landscape architect's palette is more varied and provocative than that offered to any other designer. He has the benefit of the best of man's efforts in architecture, horticulture, and the fine arts; and he has the materials and resources of the natural world at his disposal.

Sculpture is one of the most pleasant of man-made additions to be used in our gardens. It can be modern, a copy of an Oriental goddess, or an Italian maiden newly escaped from a Renaissance garden.

Photograph by Pam-Anela Messenger

Scale in garden sculpture is important. A sculpture should be large enough to be seen but not so large that it overshadows your plantings. The mood, your income, and the scale will all influence your choice. Whatever you select, it should be something you like and it should belong in the setting created for it.

Photograph by Maynard L. Parker

In garden design, either may come first—the
setting for the sculpture you already have or
a piece of sculpture to complete the niche
designed as a point of interest in the garden.

After greenery, nothing, I believe, enhances a garden more than sculpture. Unlike flowers, it survives the changing seasons yet is not unchanging, for most sculpted materials not only weather but alter their appearance dramatically in different lights.

Sculpture, statuary, wall plaques, and ceramics are not used enough in gardens, either through a fear of seeming pretentious or a lack of realization of what art can mean in the general composition.

The old concept that statuary should dominate the area or should be at the end of every main axis and cross axis doesn't apply any more. It can be used casually on a wall or to brighten a corner of the garden.

Photograph by Pam-Anela Messenger

Trees Can Be Living Sculpture

Look carefully at your trees to be sure you have developed all they
have to give you. Their beauty is not in foliage alone but in their
shape and branching and in the relation of their structure to their
foliage. It's pleasant and exciting to look up into a tree and through a
tree as well as at it.

Pruning shears, wisely used, are the gardener's best friend.

Photograph by Maynard L. Parker

"Trees already grown are invaluable. To
have them, or not to have them is, to
speak in a business phrase, to begin
with capital or without it."
ROBERT SOUTHEY, The Doctor, 1834

"'Trimming up' instead of cutting out
is the common error of persons ignorant
of the arts of sylvan picture making."
F.J. SCOTT, Suburban Home Grounds,
1870

"Some Ignorants are against pruning,
suffering their trees to run and ramble
to such a head of confusion, as neither
bears well nor fair."
JOHN REID, The Scots Gardener, 1683

This covered walkway illustrates not only the value of trimming trees to open a view, but also the decorative value of branch structure in a garden composition.

A Tree Makes the New Look Old

Unlike people, gardens never strive for perpetual youth—they want to look old from the day they were born. Their greatest beauty comes with maturity. New gardens try to look old before their time. They are in luck when old trees exist to help them out—even one tree of scale and stature will give a garden a semblance of middle age before its first birthday.

To both the designer and garden lover, however, certain species, regardless of size, come as mixed blessings. The native California bay shown here was such a tree. If it were to survive civilization in the new garden, certain long-acquired habits would have to be respected. Being used to winter rains and summer drought, it wouldn't tolerate a lot of water, while paving too close to its trunk would stifle the root system.

If the owner were to cherish it, rather than chop it down within six months, certain faults would have to be accepted and coped with. All evergreen trees shed a few leaves a day for exercise, but a bay tree excels in being difficult. It fights captivity, has messy flowers, drips oil, welcomes pests and disease, and is unfriendly to other plants if they get too near.

A redwood platform—octagon-shaped and 26 feet across—was chosen as the design element most sympathetic to these limitations. It reflects and increases the tree's dominance, is visually pleasant, can be used as a garden seat or buffet, and has even been a bandstand for music at a party and a terrace on which a bride and groom cut the cake.

On the practical side, the deck allows for controlled watering of the tree and permits air to reach its roots; the paving stops just inside the shadow line. The leaves and their inevitable stain blend with the dark wood, while grass and other plantings keep a safe distance.

Yet, without this one old tree, difficult as it was to please, the garden would have an entirely different feeling. It would take many years to approach the character pictured here, photographed after a sweeping but before the garden was two years old.

Serene and majestic in its domination of the area, the old California bay tree adds maturity to a newly created garden.

Patterns

OPPOSITE: Flanking a garden entrance, stalks of Isabella grapes are trimmed bare, with the foliage stapled along the wall top. A privet hedge is at the base.

OPPOSITE, LEFT: Algerian ivy trained on wire forms an allover diamond pattern which lasts the year round.

OPPOSITE, RIGHT: Trained on a thick wire in 30-inch squares, an espaliered *Grewia caffra* casts a bold, year-round pattern.

BELOW: A striking pattern applied to an otherwise blank wall.

"To fill that space with objects of beauty, to delight the eye after it has been struck, to fix the attention where it has been caught, to prolong astonishment into admiration, are purposes not unworthy of the greatest designs."
HUMPHRY REPTON, *Sketches and Hints on Landscape Gardening*, 1795

Trees Are for Shadow

To list the endless fascinations of trees would be a volume in itself, but not the least of them is the shadows they cast. Against buildings, onto the terrace, and across the lawn they provide a moving silhouette, varying in intensity, changing every hour.

Whether broadleaf or conifer, deciduous or evergreen, their shadows are soft and clustered at noon, long and dramatic at sundown— needed for shade, welcomed for pattern.

Hedging

Crisp, controlled hedges add strength and style to a garden, but only if they're the right scale and properly placed.

For the patient gardener, there's a long list of hedge material which time and care will develop into structural horizontals of green. The impatient can install a frame of chain-link fencing at whatever height they want their hedge to be and plant ivy. In several growing seasons the frame-work is covered and the desired effect is achieved.

The choice will depend on the color and texture the gardener wants the hedge to be, his budget, and his patience or lack of it. Many people say, "Don't give me hedges that have to be clipped all the time." Actually, most hedges can be maintained in half a day two or three times a year.

A controlled hedge can solve an infinite number of landscaping problems, from a need for privacy to adding textural and structural interest.

It is a year-round green fence, a separator of areas, a screen against the house next door, a stage setting for flowers, and a windscreen.

Make It Geometric

No one can deny the perfection of the French château garden as its hedges twist and turn in an endless variation of classic patterns called "parterres." Parterres are first an overall geometric design, resting calmly in a designated space. Closer observation reveals a rhythmic play of squares and circles, cubes, spheres, and spirals, combining into intricate patterns.

Parterres are intriguing; they hold the viewer's interest as he mentally traces the curves, remembering perhaps his old geometry lessons. Aesthetically aware, he will be excited by the relationships of forms which the designer has established.

Here at home, we return to our European heritage in planning our gardens and often recall these parterres. On a modest scale, they are suitable to our half-day-a-week gardening help. They are, in fact, ideal for this kind of care.

Biannual pruning will maintain their form and good looks. Usually of evergreen materials—the greens of boxwood and euonymus or the grays of santolina and teucrium—they are suitable to many climatic conditions.

Complicated in appearance, the precision of the design and the carefully pruned look can be achieved with a minimum of care and effort.

Photograph by Maynard L. Parker

The Naturalness of Stone

The character of a garden stairway is determined to a great extent by the material used in its construction.

When a designer wants a natural-looking flight of steps, as opposed to a frankly formal and architectural one, he thinks of stone as it occurs in nature—waterworn or weathered, warm in color, and with a possible patina of lichen. He knows that such stone collaborates with the mason's skill in creating a stairway in sympathy with its surroundings.

Stone and Wood Combine to Make Steps

The Stone Stairway

An integral part of the wall it climbs, this stairway allows for access to the upper terrace without destroying the beauty of the wall itself when viewed from the lower garden. One may ignore railings when the change in grade is no more than 4½ feet.

Since stone is a natural complement to plants, their use in the stairway itself heightens the recall of a natural scene.

Pockets of topsoil, provided while the steps are being built, assure proper growing conditions. Planning ahead is important but doesn't have to be obvious in the final effect.

Plants soften a stairway when used along each side. The texture of the foliage contrasts with the surface of the stone and each is enhanced by the comparison.

Photograph by Rondal Partridge

Plants in the Landscape

Trees, shrubs, vines, ground covers, and grasses cover much of the earth; knowing them and how to use them is what distinguishes the landscape architect from those in closely related fields of design.

Plants are a link with our primeval past. They offer us shade and shadow, shelter and sustenance and give us color, texture, form, and mass to work with in man-made compositions. Beyond this, they grow, burst into flower, drop their leaves, change color, and bear fruit.

They are a friend to man (possible exceptions, poison ivy and barrel cactus) and can be transplanted thousands of miles from their native habitat or grown for years confined in a pot for man's pleasure.

They bear no resentment when severely cut; they come back again and again when constantly sheared and collaborate willingly when man's fancy turns them into pleached allées, pyramids, spirals, or peacocks.

By their shape, color, and foliage texture, plants show that they are intended to enhance architecture, not hide or compete with it. Vines can soften its lines, plants can create a base for it, and trees can frame it; for all are, in fact, only part of a larger design concept.

One plant well chosen can improve a composition, where ten—fighting for light and air—more often result in confusion.

Photograph by Maynard L. Parker

Photograph by Maynard L. Parker

Plant to Screen Your Window

Time and again the picture window performs only the function of allowing the neighbors to see into your living room. Pulling the shades seems to be a contradiction to the picture window idea, so what can a home owner do?

Plants with color and character help screen the window without shutting off the entire view. The design of the walk and the variety of plantings will help to keep your neighbors more interested in the garden than in you.

In the photograph, the heaviest screen element is the group of New Zealand flax (*Phormium tenax*) planted far enough out to look well from the windows. Contrasting with this are groups of European white birch (*Betula pendula alba*), which stay light and airy. Clusters of blue and white agapanthus and the gray-foliaged dusty miller with yellow flowers complete the planting.

Paving

Paving—something hard and convenient under foot—has been man's concern ever since he came down out of the trees.

Paving to keep his feet dry—paving to pull his chariots over—paving to accommodate mobs of people—paving to walk on in a garden.

The cobblestones of Europe represent centuries of labor by men determined to pull themselves out of the mud of the Middle Ages. Their patterns, from the bold cobblestones of the Paris streets to the pebble mosaics of Spain, have been an inspiration to all garden designers.

Paving must be sympathetic with the grass, trees, and flowers upon whose domain it has encroached and must set them off to their best advantage. They will in turn enhance the paving by softening its outlines and casting shadows across it.

Paving leaves less area for planting, and since there are fewer plants, they should be selected with more care and cared for with more enthusiasm.

If complicated paving patterns and colors are introduced into an already exciting composition, the resulting confusion, rivaling Joseph's coat, may be a constant irritation.

It may be the role of paving to remain calm, to be the common denominator and a foil for the excitement created by fences, steps, grass forms, brilliant flower combinations, foliage textures, and distant views.

Photograph by Carolyn Caddes

Paving Makes Year-Round Pattern

Paving is one of the major design elements in the garden. Different materials may be combined in an infinite variety of patterns to satisfy the designer and intrigue the observer.

Paving is not necessarily just a terrace plus a network of paths leading to various parts of the garden. It may cover large areas and hold within itself plots of grass and flowers, trees, rock outcroppings and pools.

Paving cannot substitute for the expanse of open lawn on a large property, but the relative proportion of paving to grass can often be increased with good results. In hot or subtropical climates, large paved areas will radiate too much heat unless shaded; but for the average house on a small lot the amount of paving can be greatly increased without robbing us of the fundamental pleasures of a garden.

Stockholm

New York

Villa d'Este

All Brick Paving

A grass panel becomes the terrace outside this garden room. Paths, mowing strips, and loggia paving are of brick. The boxwood and ivy are permanent and always green.

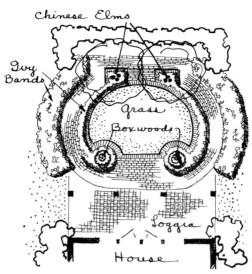

Photograph by Fred Lyon

Photograph by Maynard L. Parker

An Octagonal Design

The small courtyard at the back of an art gallery required an elegant treatment—why not decorate the floor? With an eight-pointed star design in concrete paving, using natural stone colors—beige, charcoal, and gray—a small fountain on one wall, an 18-inch-high bench against the other, and minimum planting, little else is needed to furnish this city retreat.

Water in the Garden

The garden pool means hard work. It must be kept clean and well-groomed. You might consider using water-worn stone as the material to define the form. Beautifully weathered and large in scale, such stone blends with other natural materials to create a quiet and restful composition. These stones can be laid with topsoil so that planting may soften the lines.

The fun is in deciding where moss and alpines will "occur" without obscuring the dominant strength of the form and the material used.

Illustrated is a traditional ornamental pool, constructed with natural stone steps leading down to the water, containing plants and serving as a habitat for goldfish.

Photograph by Michael La

Photograph by Carolyn Caddes

The driveway to this elegant house was rerouted to encircle the lake. The first glimpse of the building is now across the mirrorlike body of water, which reflects the trees and the sky.

A body of water makes a good garden boundary, as evidenced in the moats surrounding the old castles and châteaux.

To make a calm and fitting foreground for the mountain range visible in the distance, a pool was built at the rim of the small garden illustrated. The water follows the base of the retaining wall and visually enlarges the small area, which might otherwise be diminished by the strength of the backdrop.

The Villa d'Este at Tivoli is not only a complete water garden to be seen but a vast, rumbling organ as well. Ingenious devices were used to churn and agitate the water in numerous fountains and cascades.

"After you have laid out the great walls
and chief defigns you may furnish the
rest of your garden with feveral different
defigns as Tall groves, Quincunxes,
Galleries and Halls of Verdure,
Labyrinths, Bowling greens, and
Amphitheatres adorned with fountains.
All these works distinguish a garden
from what is common and contribute
not a little to render it magnificent."

ALEXANDER LEBLOND,
The Theory and Practice of Gardening,
1728

THOMAS CHURCH, 1974.

Swimming in the Garden

T he pool is a place to gather around, much as a fireplace is in a room. It offers swimming for the athlete or just getting wet if you are hot.

It can remain a simple reflection pool in the garden in which you occasionally take a dip or become a complete entertainment center where you have as many fascinations for children and guests as you can dream up. It may have a cabana with shade and lemonade, or maybe a bar. It might have a soda fountain and a sandwich counter. If your guests stay for the weekend, it can double as a guest house.

If you think you will want a pool some time in the future, let it be part of your master plan now, so you won't put large, immovable objects where the pool should be. Think of the grades, the orientation for sun and shade and protection from wind. Think of access for the pool contractor, who would like to bring a loader and trucks right up to the pool area. You will need some paved area around the pool for sunbathing and furniture; the filter and heater must be housed, and storage room for equipment and cushions is a sound idea.

Most people request a pool which will be convenient and useful and so conceived as to look well the year round within a larger design concept. Often the designer finds that the standard rectangular or classic forms are not to his liking, and he strikes out into the exciting (but dangerous) area of curved, angular, or nonobjective art forms. Many designers, dictated by the available space and contours of the site and informed by a knowledge of scale and proportion, are highly successful.

The private swimming pool, once a luxury for the few, seems to be here to stay for the many.

Pool in the Landscape

This garden for a modern house in Santa Barbara, California, recalls the simplicity and scale of classic European gardens. Yet the only immigrants are the Italian maidens, who were given one-way tickets from Florence to their present abode. Silhouetted against the trees and mountains, they contribute to the strength and interest of the composition. (Try blocking them out and see how lonely the whole garden becomes.)

While perhaps this isn't a scheme many of us can have, it does illustrate several important principles of garden design. It is often true that an exciting view of powerful background needs a compelling accent in the foreground to give depth, at the same time relating it to human scale and the people experiencing it. Also, it goes without saying that a mean dimension looks that much meaner placed against a great panorama, so the scale of the terrace becomes more important than the material from which it is built or the uses to which it is put.

While the swimming pool is very simple, it is decorative all year long and is an integrated element of the spacious terrace.

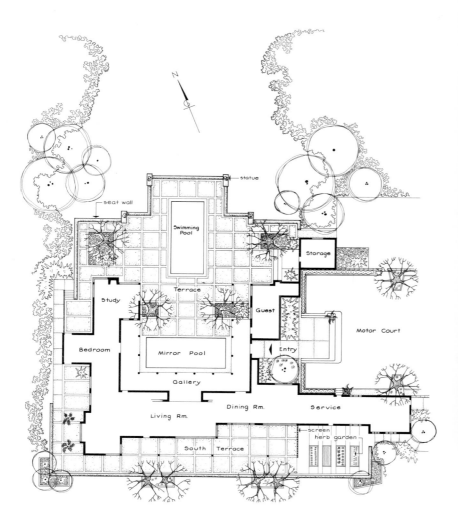

Photograph by Maynard L. Parker

In the Utah Mountains

The problem here was clearly not space! It was that a suitable site was some distance from the house. The pavilion and terrace solved it.

Sensitively sited in an oak forest some distance from the house, the swimmers in this 44-foot circular pool enjoy a panoramic view.

The simple shapes are well integrated with the gently sloping ground and the natural setting.

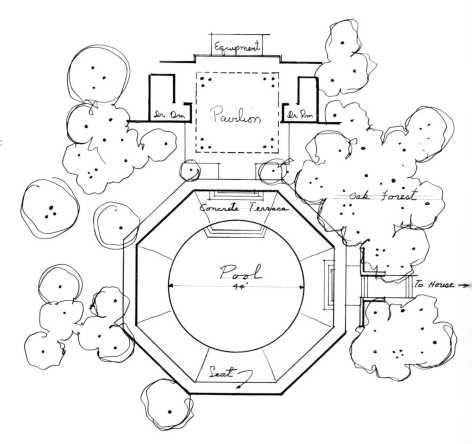

Photograph by John D. Eccles

Swimming in the Garden / 135

With a Pool for Children

A covered, open-sided bridge divides the
swimming pool into two areas. One, within
easy reach of the house, is a shallow pool for
children; the other, whose surrounding
terrace overlooks the valley and distant hills,
is for more experienced swimmers.

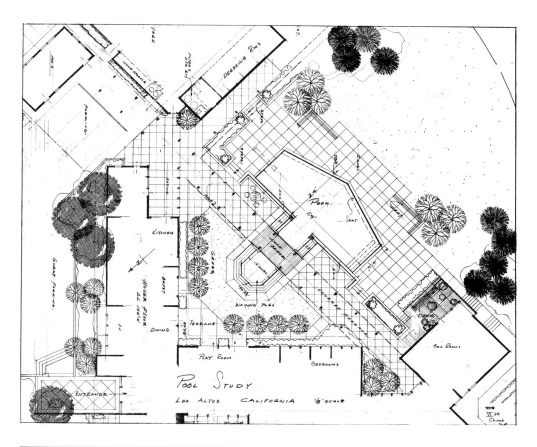

POOL STUDY

LOS ALTOS   CALIFORNIA   ⅛" SCALE

In a Redwood Clearing

The house and swimming pool were built on the site of an old northern California estate which had been subdivided. The construction of the original garden dates back to the time when Chinese labor crews were building the west's railroads. Evidence of this can be seen in the high stone wall adjacent to the house. New walls, built of the same stone, retain the hillside around the pool and tie in the new with the old. Vinca and rosemary cover the banks with crisp green and silver foliage and blue flowers.

The position of the pool was chosen on the basis of the best sun exposure; it was cantilevered over the canyon at the far end, and dressing rooms hidden from view were installed beneath the structure.

Photograph by Michael L.

At first glance the pool seems to be a simple
rectangle; in fact, the end nearer the house is
the wider of the two, the result being that the
pool appears to be a great deal longer than it
actually is. A diving board was installed to
meet the requirements of a young family.

otograph by Michael Laurie

Swimming Pool with Spa

This seemingly large area appeared to offer a multitude of possibilities for siting the house and garden. The owner's program included a ranch-style house, tennis court, terraces, swimming pool, and spa. Existing views, sun and wind patterns, a natural drainage swale, large oaks, and local building ordinances all affected the final location of the house and swimming pool.

On this property, space for a swimming pool was not a problem. The problem was its relationship to the house and the rest of the garden. If, for convenience, the pool were to be placed a few steps away from the house, it would be partially shaded six months of the year. But for an active young family an extra walk for a swim would not be a hardship, and besides, the noise generated by young pool activists at a distance would be that much further removed from the study.

Free-form in shape, the pool occupies a central position in the garden and meets the owner's distance requirements for swimming laps. A spa is fitted neatly into one arm of the pool, and, in spite of the pool's central location, a sense of privacy from the house is obtained by placement of large, river-washed stones and plantings.

To compensate for winter shade on the areas adjacent to the house, a breakfast terrace was extended to poolside, sufficiently away from the house to receive the winter sun.

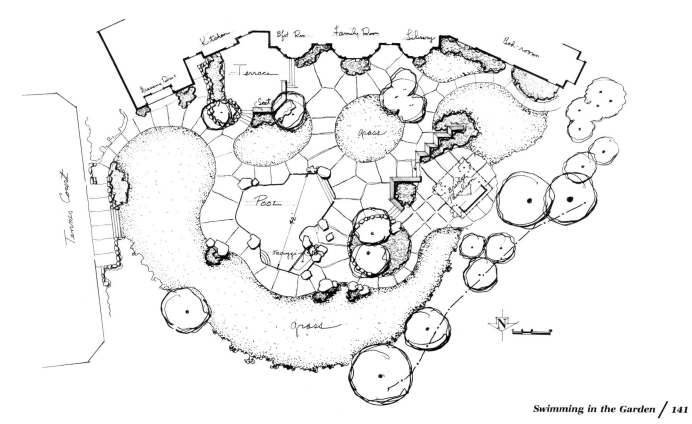

Kitchen Bfst Rm Family Room Library Bed-room

Dressing Room Terrace

Seat

grass

Tennis Court

Pool

Jacuzzi

grass

N

A circular shape was the choice here in this pleasant sylvan setting. Edged with a rock retaining wall, the pool is situated on the lowest level of a hillside garden, in a clearing of a eucalyptus grove.

The Shape of Pools

The questions of the size and shape of the pool and surrounding areas need thought and coordination before the hole is dug. Being the largest single design element in the composition, the pool cannot be hidden or disregarded on properties of an acre or less. Its success or failure, aesthetically, will depend on where it is placed, what forms are chosen as being most sympathetic to the site, what materials will do the most to heighten possible dramatic effects and blend most harmoniously with the house and the distant landscape. If the whole garden area is to become primarily a swimming club for your family and friends, the influence of the pool and its surroundings will involve the house and terraces in its scope and activity and will reach to the property lines.

There is no fixed rule about what shape a pool should be. The shape may be influenced by your own convictions and prejudices. It may be determined by how many children you have, how far they want to swim, and how deep they want to dive. Rectangles, circles, ovals, classic shapes, and a free form may all be possibilities. Site restrictions and your reason for wanting a pool will influence its size and shape.

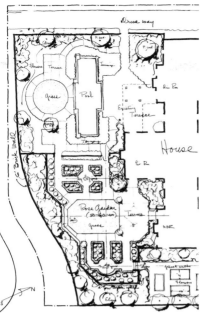

Forty Feet Long and Ten Feet Wide

This pool in Hillsborough, California was added long after the garden was established and was not intended to have a functional look.

Relieving the pool's long, narrow shape, shallow steps lead down to the water from the terrace. They are balanced on the other side by a break in the coping. Flowering annuals surrounding the pool provide color, and statues representing the four seasons line one edge.

The pool rests comfortably in the whole composition, and 40 feet of water gives the swimmers ample space.

© Photograph by Morley Baer

Free-Form Pool

On this flat, level area a free-form pool complements the landscape setting for a contemporary house (1975). The pool plaster is black to give the illusion of depth to the water, and the coping is of natural stones to blend with the large rocks placed around the pool.

Rectangular Pool

An oblong pool fits well into this level site, formerly a lawn at the rear of the house. A seat wall, built of brick, edges one side and encircles the far end of the pool, giving a balance to the lawn opposite and a height variation on an otherwise flat area.

Photograph by Michael Laurie

Photograph by Carolyn Caddes

Circular Pool

Like a swimming hole in the mountains, this circular pool high above the Pacific Ocean is integrated into its natural setting with rough stone paving and rocks. The joyful sculpture reflects the mood of this garden.

Trefoil Pool

In this verdant setting a cloverleaf shape was chosen. The coping is of brick, matching the surrounding seat wall. Four raised planters at the pool's edge hold pink and white geraniums. The shape provides a good length for swimmers and a shallow alcove for bathers.

Photograph by Michael Laurie

Photograph by Carolyn Caddes

Photograph by Otto Lang

On a Rolling Foothill Site

The southern orientation of this house and
garden takes full advantage of the dramatic
vista toward the coastal mountain range while
incorporating several large, existing live oaks
into the house-entry and pool-terrace areas.

The owner wanted a low-maintenance garden
with a swimming pool, looking like a natural
pond, as a focal point.

Seventy tons of river-washed sandstone rocks
were placed around the pool area. The pool
plaster is black, and the surrounding plants
are native to the area, requiring minimum
maintenance.

The rolling grass appears to extend into the
distant trees; in reality, the owner's vegetable
garden lies just beyond the crest, taking full
advantage of the southern exposure.

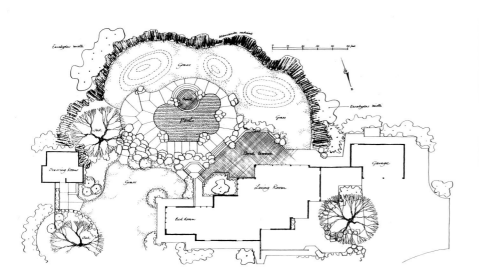

Above, the site under construction. The grass area was elevated, forming mounds to blend with the curves of the pool.

Photograph by Carolyn Caddes

© *Photograph by Morley Baer*

In an Oriental Style

Designed for an oriental-style house, the free form of this pool evokes a Japanese garden while at the same time accommodating swimming, diving, and jacuzzi relaxation. The gardenesque quality of the pool is enhanced by the use of black plaster and the incorporation of rocks and planting at the edge.

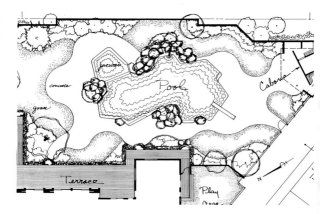

Photograph by Michael Laurie

Formal Pool in a Courtyard Setting

In this enclosed courtyard the swimming pool is the center attraction. On one side, facing the house, is a pavilion containing a pool equipment area and dressing rooms (Figs. 1 and 3). The architecture is reminiscent of Versailles' buildings of the seventeenth century.

In keeping with the precise symmetry and detailing of the architecture, the planting around the pool is formally arranged in tubs and urns. A stone cherub stands on the coping at each of the pool's four corners, and twin fountains play on either side of the pavilion, a pleasant bonus for both eye and ear.

A soft, muted rose, accented by a white trim, is the color chosen for the buildings. Three shades of pink geraniums in the decorative urns echo the rose of the walls. An interesting planting detail is the tubbed Indian laurel (*Ficus refusa*, Fig. 3) at each of the four curves in the pool's coping. They are miniatures of the ficus standing at either side of the house.

1

3

Photographs by Michael Laurie

A Swimming Pool Built on Rocky Terrain

On this steep and wooded site, with views through the trees to the Pacific Ocean, the pool was constructed on the lower of two terraces at the rear of the house.

In making a clearing for this pool, as many trees as possible were saved. The terrace, which surrounds the pool, floats into the forest and is paved with three shades of red brick in a herringbone pattern. The pool is edged with a double row of the same brick.

Redwood benches, iron railings, and concrete planter boxes contrast with the greens of the water and foliage.

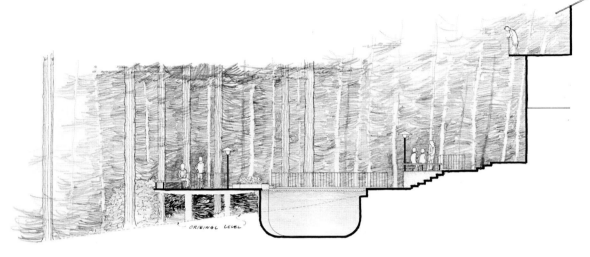

ORIGINAL LEVEL

Photographs by Michael Laurie

© Photograph by Morley Baer

In a Wooded Area

The original site for this house and garden, with excellent native California live oaks, sloped toward a heavily wooded ravine. To establish a close relationship with the natural setting, a free-form swimming pool was suggested, but it was decided that a calm, self-contained circle (also a form found in nature) would rest more easily on the site.

The slope between the house and the pool area was retained with large slabs of river-washed stone, through which a stream trickles and splashes. Stepping down to the pool, the stones form a waterfall, a small

pool, and plant pockets for azaleas, ferns, a Japanese maple, and other shade-loving colorful shrubs and flowers.

The pool coping and terrace are of buff-colored brick, in contrast to the gray and brown of the redwood house and pavilion. The pool plaster is green, which gives it depth and a sylvan quality.

The house and deck overlook the pool and garden pavilion. The pool is obviously man-made, but it is sympathetic to the natural surroundings, and the visual transition to the surrounding landscape is effortless.

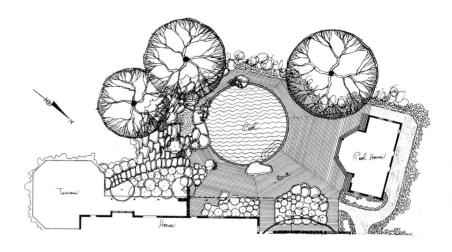

A Pool Garden in Florida

This classical pool was sited between the house and the shore of Hobe Sound, Florida.

Viewed from the terrace the sound can be seen through a clearing in the original vegetation, with an outsize banyan tree dominating the lawn area. Retaining walls set off the pool and terrace from nature; however, light and clouds reflect in the pool, relating the whole in a pleasing scene. Top left, page 155, shows the site before the pool was built and the lawns planted.

Photographs by Margaret Blair

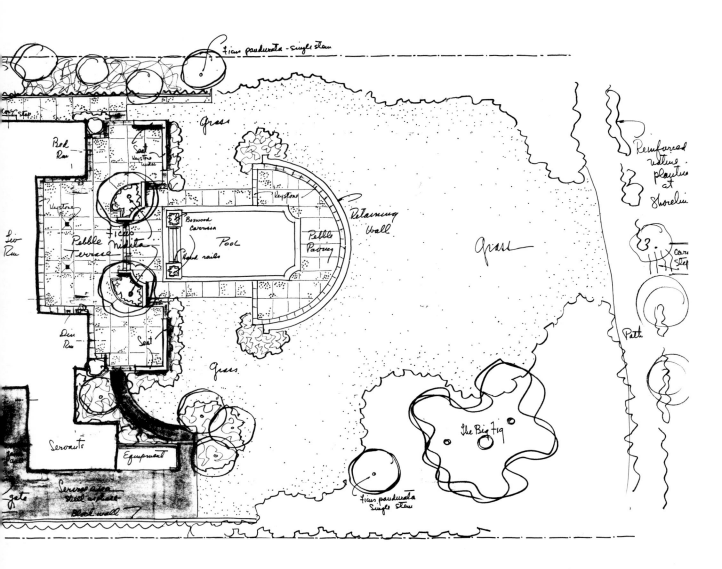

In a Clearing

By incorporating the natural rocks and leaving native plants and live oaks untouched, the problem of projecting this pool and pool house into the landscape without destroying it was solved.

The pool reflects the rustic cabana (opposite), oriented toward the view.

Photographs by Michael Laurie.

Before and After

When redesigning a garden, one usually has to try to blend the new harmoniously with the old.

Before the pool was installed, these curving steps were a feature leading down to a long stretch of lawn. In making them part of the pool structure, the arcs of the steps were used to determine the shape of the pool.

The symmetry of the garden is retained, with the substitution of a swimming pool in place of the lawn.

Photographs by Maynard L. Parker

A Sculptured Island
in the Pool

Originally it was planned to use one of the
big boulders from the site as a play island in
the pool. This was changed (the rough rock
would have torn the swimmers to pieces) into
an island of concrete, designed by sculptor
Adaline Kent.

It separates the swimming and play areas and
is a center of fun for divers and underwater
experts, who swim through a hole in the
base. Like most islands these days, it's usually
crowded with sunbathers.

Photograph by Michael Laurie

© *Photograph by Morley Baer*

A Garden Tour

T*he gardens you will see in this chapter range from small town gardens to fairly large (for today's standards) country places. The tour will include modest gardens for tract houses, remodeled gardens for old houses, and more elaborate schemes where space and funds were not limited.*

You will be shown the owner's problems, desires, and the final solutions.

When the tour is over, may you feel that having a garden is a pleasure and that gardening, to whatever degree you indulge in it, is rewarding.

7

"A city garden, especially of one who has no other, ought to be planted and ornamented with all possible care."
CATO, 234– 149 B.C.

"I never had any other desire so strong, and so like to Covetousness, as . . . that I might be master at last of a small house and large Garden, with very moderate conveniences joined to them . . ."
ABRAHAM COWLEY, *The Garden*, 1664

Town and Country Gardens

Expanded Toward the Street

Prior to remodeling, this house, with a nondescript kind of step and an untidy front lawn, was exposed to the street, which was 16 feet away.

Now, a brick wall ensures privacy from the sidewalk. A row of clipped sycamores cuts out the view from the neighbor's house across the street, and a pleasant, quiet, sheltered garden is the result.

New doors and wide steps provide access from the house (Fig. 2). Try covering two-thirds of the width of these steps and it is soon apparent what an improvement the expansive touch of extra footage is. The entrance from the street is formalized and now looks as if it belongs to the aristocratic home. It is screened from the patio, but a glimpse of the adjoining area makes both seem more spacious. A small space between the top of the brick wall and the leaves of the plane trees is the secret of the feeling of openness in this garden.

Figures 4 through 8 show the garden twenty-five years later. Careful pruning has kept the line of the pleached sycamores.

Northern California, 1955

1

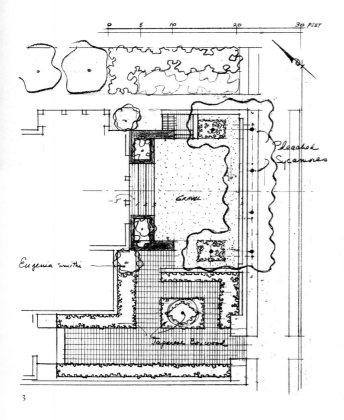

3

2

Photographs by Maynard L. Parker

4

5

6

7

Photographs by Carolyn Caddes

Northern California, 1980

Intriguing Curves Enhance Small Backyard

There was nothing very wrong with the backyard shown in the picture (Fig. 1), but nothing very right, either. Walks were angular and led nowhere in particular. The corner at the rear was overgrown and without character.

The concrete was replaced with brick laid in pleasing curves, and the back corner was cleared out. This revealed the wall, which has good character.

Now the quiet, secluded garden, accented by the vivid colors of flowers in the sunshine and by the contrasts of textures and form, looks well in all seasons and is easily maintained (Fig. 2).

Palo Alto, California, 1964

1

2

Back to Front

When the owners purchased this house, there was a redwood forest in front and the driveway curved around the building to a garage in the back garden (Fig. 1).

In a few months many changes were made. A number of trees were removed, but those remaining gave a feeling of privacy and luxurious growth.

An open carport was designed around one of the redwoods in the front, thus blending it unobtrusively into the garden.

What was once the driveway is now a handsome swimming pool, with a cool green color, a curved design to conform to the space of the back garden, and a brick edging to harmonize with the terrace above (Figs. 2 and 3). The former garage was converted into an open lanai.

Palo Alto, California, 1968

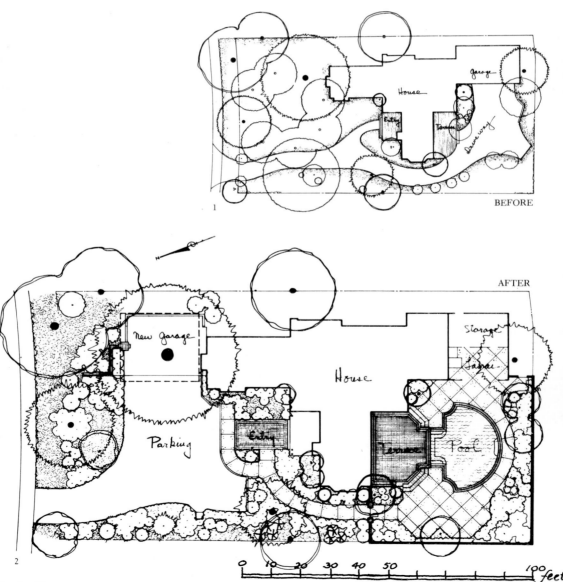

1   BEFORE

AFTER

2

3

Photograph by Carolyn Caddes

Backyard Treasures

One of the rewards of buying an old house is the unexpected pleasure of uncovering the treasures which may be buried in the garden.

The owners of this house found a fortune in old trees, which money can't buy, full-grown boxwood hedges (not often available and always expensive), and urns which had miraculously remained intact. These treasures were used to develop the garden illustrated here. Because it is a south garden, the owners moved their living room to the back of the house so they could overlook and enjoy the garden's pattern and reach it easily when they were in search of a quiet retreat.

San Francisco, California, 1957

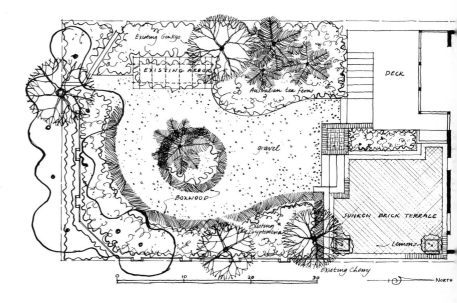

Photographs by Bruce Harlow

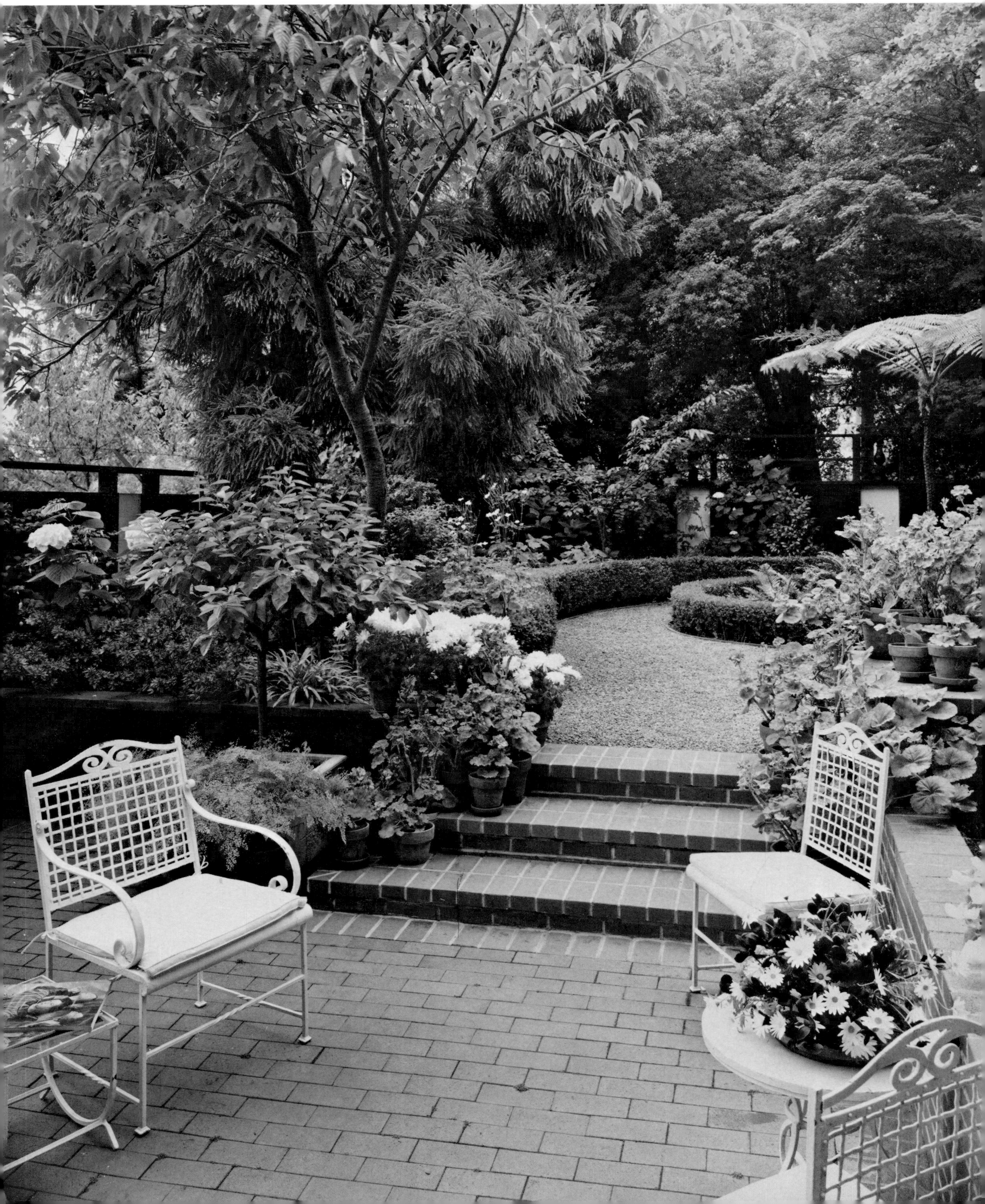

A Garden with Symmetry and Motion

The garden illustrated here is to be seen from a second-story living room rather than used constantly. It makes use of strong, year-round pattern in paving, walls, and planting, with a minimum of seasonal color.

Each one of the four designs (bottom) was considered for this small area before the final choice was made (below).

San Francisco, California, 1935

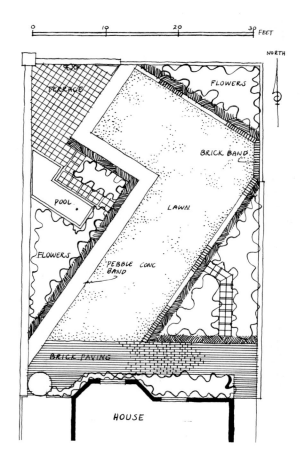

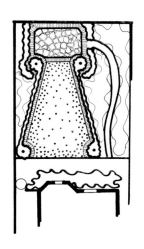

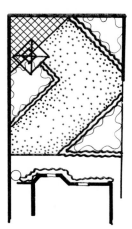

Photographs by Rondal Partridge

Limited Space

Many people want—on a small lot—what used to be on an estate. This is a lot 100 by 120 feet. The owners needed a two-car garage and a place for guests to park. They wanted a swimming pool, terraces to entertain lots of people, a vegetable garden, trees and planting, and an arbor so they could eat outside in the shade. It all got there without seeming too crowded. The pool is raised because the land was high. Two sides have no path around the pool, which saves space. The garden is a series of outdoor rooms. The pool is decorated with tile collected in Spain.

Atherton, California, 1961

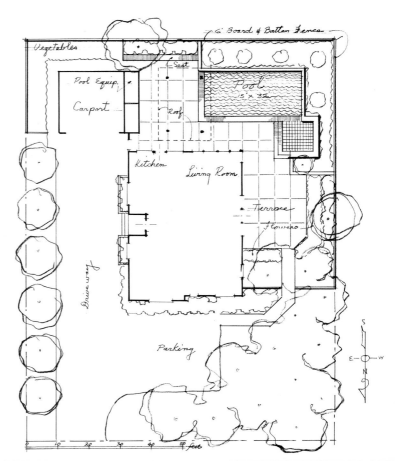

Suburban Tract

This house, like thousands of others, was ordinary but sound (Fig. 1). The lot was good but uncultivated and unfenced from the neighbors on either side. The original driveway was straight and narrow. Visitors had to park on the street, and the owners often had to walk on wet grass to get past their car and reach the front door. Now the generous curve of the extended drive adds beauty to the house. Color is added in the center bed by clusters of blue and white agapanthus, and gray-foliaged dusty miller with yellow flowers, in the raised bed at the right (Fig. 2).

A group of New Zealand flax (*Phormium tenax*) is planted far enough out to look well from the window. Contrasting with it are groups of European white birch (*Betula pendula alba*), which stays light and airy. Figure 4 shows the garden twenty-five years later.

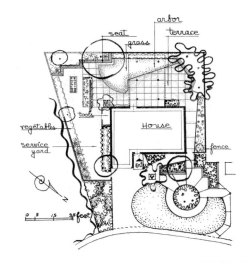

1

Photograph by Maynard L. Parker

2

Photograph by Carolyn Caddes

4

Photograph by Maynard L. Parker

3

The picture window at the back of the house (Fig. 6) had no protection from a bright western sun. The blinds had to be drawn each day until the sun went down. To control this problem, a sunshade was designed to extend from the house to the lot line 32 feet away (Fig. 7). The first section is solid to shade the window and the rest is open lath to permit light to filter onto the pebble-concrete paving and grass.

Photograph by Maynard L. Parker

New posts were built in front of the fence so that wire could be strung along the top to support the ivy, adding a foot of screening without an obvious patch job (Fig. 10). Stained dark, the fence recedes to make the garden seem wider than it is. Built-in seating, raised beds, and a narrow but long grass form also add to the space illusion.

Palo Alto, California, 1951

Photograph by Rondal Partridge

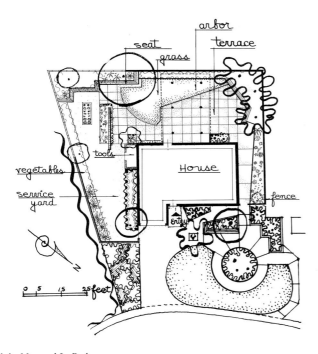

arbor
seat
grass
terrace
tools
vegetables
service yard
House
fence
entry

0 5 15 25 feet

N

Mid City

This backyard (Fig. 1) was ready to be remodeled into a garden.

As the focal point, a baroque design was chosen for the pool; its curves follow those of the door and window at the rear of the Victorian house (Fig. 3). A functional terrace with hexagonal paving surrounds the pool and establishes the garden as an extension of the house (Fig. 5). Three main elements—evergreens, stonework, and water, the essence of all Italian gardens—now combine with the strong geometric forms to suggest a classical European garden.

The new carport and arbor structures, along with existing plant materials, create privacy from the neighboring apartment to the east (Fig. 4). A small vegetable and flower garden occupies the sunny corner on the west side.

San Francisco, California, 1974

1

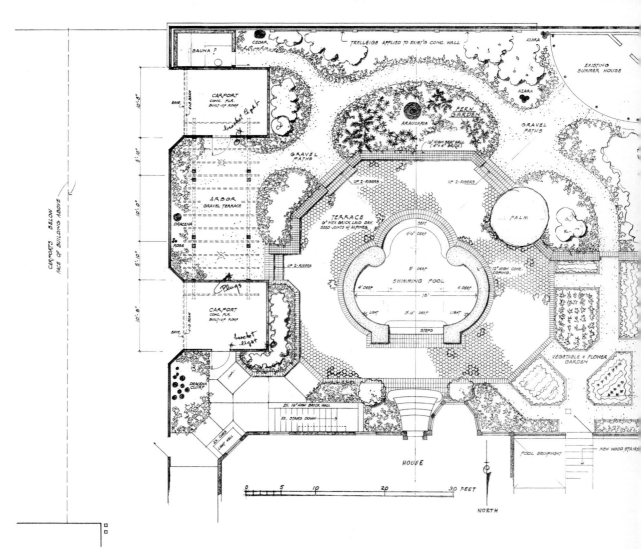

3

Photographs by Carolyn Caddes

4

5

In the Hills of Northern California

At the end of a long, winding approach through the hilly, oak-studded, grassland landscape of San Francisco's Bay Area, the visitor arrives at a spacious entrance parking court. It is protected from the wind by the surrounding native vegetation, which was retained in the design (Fig. 2).

On the south side of the house the rooms open onto a brick terrace and grass area designed around existing large, native live oaks. These extend the architectural overhang of the house and provide wind protection, shade, and foreground for the expansive view beyond. The meeting of garden and natural landscape is clearly marked by a juniper hedge (Fig. 3).

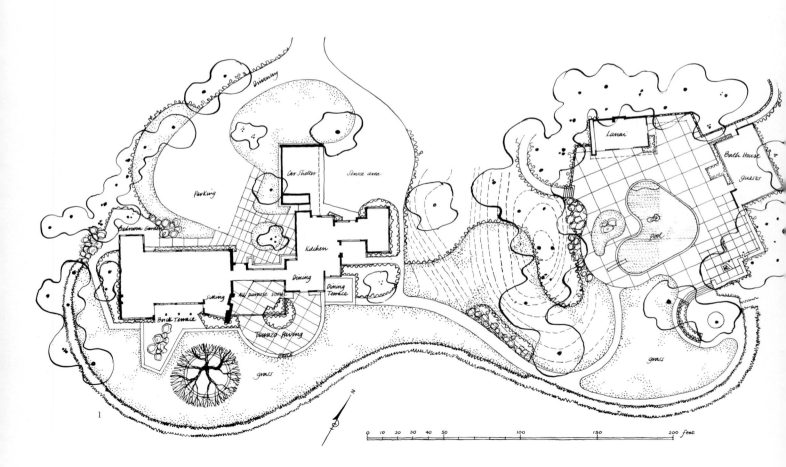

1

2

3

Photographs by Michael Laurie

The house lies below the topmost knoll. From its terraces a path curves upward and intriguingly disappears (Figs. 7 and 8) behind a rocky outcrop. It turns and arrives at the swimming pool and cabana (Fig. 6), situated below the crest.

This recreation area takes advantage of a frame of live oaks offering wind protection and shade, native boulders, and a 30-mile panoramic view of San Francisco Bay.

The pool, its shape inspired by the winding creeks of the salt marshes below, was designed to provide adequate space for all water activities. It has a shallow area for children near the recreation room, 60 feet for unobstructed swimming, and a deep section for diving.

The concrete terrace around the pool is colored tan to reduce glare. Three people are not lost on it, nor are a hundred crowded.

The cabana (Figs. 4, 5, and 6) has two sides of glass to take every advantage of the view. When the sliding doors are open, it becomes part of the terrace; a long wooden bench follows the stone wall into the room to the fireplace. By sliding the side glass door into a slot in the wall, the room may be closed and heated. (See also Chapter 6, p. 159.)   1949

4

5

Photographs by Rondal Partridge

Photograph by Michael Laurie

Photograph by Carolyn Caddes

Photograph by Michael Laurie

Top photograph by Michael Laurie; bottom photograph by Carolyn Caddes.

Santa Barbara, California

A spacious parking area and an inviting
gateway (Figs. 1 and 2) lead to the
brick-paved entry court for this charming
house in Santa Barbara. The path around the
house leads past a rock garden (Fig. 4) under
a large live oak from whose branches hang
baskets of fuchsia. Lights in the oak
illuminate the area at night.

Edged with lemon trees on one side and a
comfortable brick-paved terrace on the other,
the pool, with its underwater seating, has a
brick coping, continuing the floor patterns of
the entry court.

The tile around the waterline is a pale,
neutral color and makes the pool appear
larger than it is.

The garden was designed in 1970, and these
photographs were taken ten years later.

1

Photograph by R. Wellander

2

Photograph by G. Schumacher

3

4

Photographs 3, 4, 5, 6 by Michael Laurie

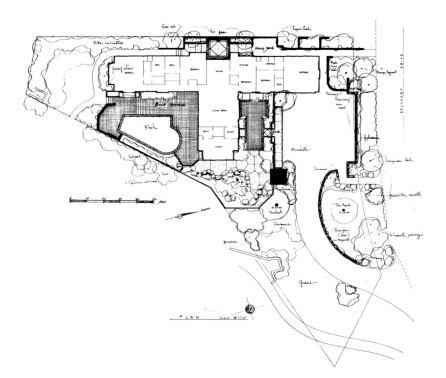

PLAN   SCALE 1/8"=1'-0"

5   6

Photographs by Carolyn Caddes

(See also page 181.)

(See also page 200.)

Photographs by Michael Laurie

Photographs by Michael Laurie

◀ (See also pages 237 and 238.)   (See also page 221.)

1

3

2

4

Two Town Gardens

Both owners of these San Francisco townhouse sites, situated side by side and sharing a fence, began with a narrow, sloping space, 17 by 52 feet. The finished gardens give privacy and are a source of beauty from all sides. Each uses different basic flooring materials, plantings, and design details to achieve its purpose.

On the left (Figs. 1 and 2), geometrics order the garden. In little space a bold statement is made. Plants were selected, placed, and trained with purpose. Deck, seating, steps and gravel are practical at ground level and interesting from above. Ivy carpets the ground and traces free-form designs on walls. Used for restrained ornamentation are Japanese maple bonsai, sculptured globes of boxwood, and yew in pots. White geraniums edge the deck.

On the right (Figs. 3 and 4) is a botanical garden: primroses, pansies, cinerarias, roses, azaleas, and camellias have burst into bloom. At three levels are a dining terrace, an octagonal deck, and an airy gazebo. Large pots of blue and white daisies are moved on occasion for bouquets at close range. Creeping thyme outlines flagstones, and steps lead to a small patio at first-floor level.

San Francisco, California, 1968

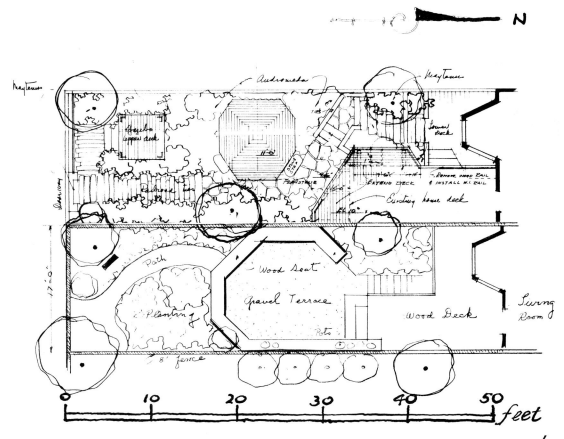

Reviving a City Backyard

A typical city backyard with a southern exposure has been changed into an area which the owners, their children, and their guests use constantly.

The original garden, a story below the dining room, was a square plot with an old shed across the rear of the property (Figs. 1, 2, and 3).

The dining-room windows are at the far left, the back porch at the right.

A wood deck, complete with built-in seats, tables, and planting pockets, was built at the dining-room level and connects with the old back porch for serving from the kitchen. French doors open onto the deck from the dining room; the fence along the side increases privacy (Figs. 4 and 5). Space for service deliveries and garbage cans is under the deck (Fig. 5).

The garden now seems twice as large, because the static lines of the original rectangle have been changed. The moving lines of the curve play against the angular forms on the opposite side (Fig. 6).

Half of the old shed was converted into a summer-house and the remainder left for tools and storage (Fig. 7).

It is now level, private, and accessible. An elm tree comes up through the deck and will provide shade and an additional screen.

San Francisco, California, 1954

"In the naive days of the old brownstone fronts, when, even if there was no daylight saving, the hours were less crowded and one could easily reach the country, the space back of these houses was given over to a wilderness of clothes lines, ashcans and prowling tomcats. It was veiled from sight by the thick draperies of the period and seen only by the servants and the ice man."
MCKENNEY AND SEYMOUR,
Your City Garden, 1937

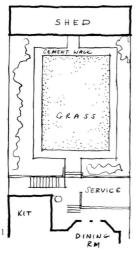

BEFORE

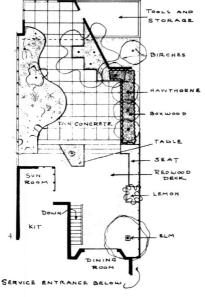

neighbor's house

AFTER

Photographs by Rondal Partridge

6

7

A City Lot, Forty by a Hundred Feet

In 1951 this hillside site was a problem. It was steep, long, narrow, and hemmed in on all sides. There were underground springs giving drainage problems.

A three-unit apartment building stands at the north end of the site. The space was terraced to give each apartment a garden.

To increase the apparent size of the narrow, rectangular space, a diagonal was cut across in the form of a privet hedge (Fig. 3).

Photographs by Pam-Anela Messenger

1

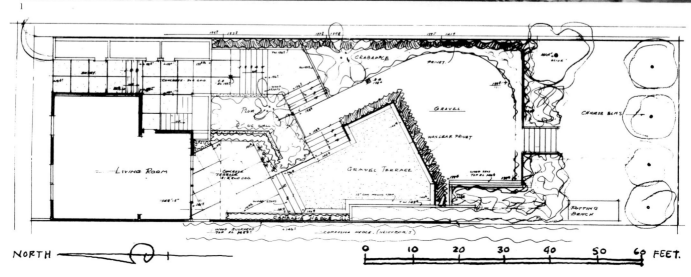

NORTH

0   10   20   30   40   50   60 FEET.

3

4

A further series of diagonals was introduced at angles to the property edges, and at each major change in level a right-angle turn was made so that no direct line through the garden remains but rather a series of traverses.

The directional changes and the changes in grade work together to form distinct areas or rooms in the garden. These rooms have different characters without detracting from the whole, because structural materials, hedges, paths, and steps are uniform throughout. Originally designed as a garden for each of the three apartments, the entire garden is now cared for by the owner. To enter, one climbs a short series of steps into the garden. A glimpse of topiary and another set of steps draw the visitor in (Fig. 1). Closest to the owner's apartment on the first level, the terrace (Fig. 5) is an extension of the living room. Tables and chairs, small-scale plants and sculpture are placed on a flooring of exposed aggregate, set diagonally to the edge of the building.

The next level is two steps down (Fig. 5) and surfaced in the fine pea gravel used in most of the garden. Here carefully pruned plants are displayed—bonsai, topiary, and urns of colorful annuals.

Three steps down and a turn to the right brings one to another terrace room (Fig. 4), at present used as a work area. Vegetables in raised beds with cold frames and more potted shrubs are cultivated here.

Another short flight of steps at the back of the garden (Fig. 3) leads to a potting shed, enclosed with hawthorn, poplar, and olive trees in an informal grouping where the land slopes gradually up to the southern boundary.

The shrubs and trees encompassing this set of outdoor rooms are relatively small, in keeping with the scale of the garden, and chosen to screen the neighboring yards and to provide windbreaks. Poplar is the largest and screens the south border. Myrtle, privet, camellia, and boxwood hedges enclose the main terrace room, define the principal diagonals of the design, and separate one area from the next.

This garden of the 1950s has had one owner in its thirty-year life. No structural changes have been made, and its geometric form is alive with imaginative plantings: rhododendron, azalea, plum, hydrangeas, camellias, roses, hawthorn, and fuchsia—a colorful display, superbly planned, organized, and maintained.

San Francisco, California, 1951

Photographs by Pam-Anela Messenger

5

Looking Toward a Wild-Flower Hillside

This design of the 1950s is an expression of the close relationship between house and garden and the use of the garden for outdoor living.

The shape of the pool, with its 45 feet of uninterrupted swimming space, exaggerates perspective, thereby increasing the apparent size of the garden as seen from the house. The pool's peninsula is large enough for a table and chairs and an umbrella.

The west boundary is defined by a natural hillside, colored by wild flowers in springtime (Fig. 3).

The four large oak trees were moved onto the site and link the garden with its setting. One's eye focuses on the oak nearest the back of the house. Three wide steps lead up to the brick-paved terrace and the wooden bench beneath, a shady place to sit and rest (Fig. 2).

Woodside, California, 1953

© *Photograph by Morley Baer*

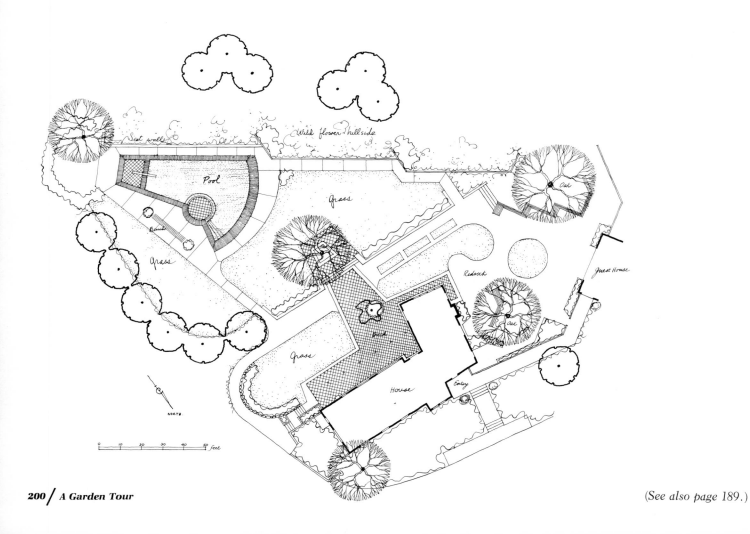

(*See also page 189.*)

Photographs by Carolyn Caddes

A Garden on the Beach

A private house on a public beach raises some problems but with a little ingenuity and planning, privacy and shelter can be achieved.

In the solution shown here, access to the beach and swimming is easy and logical. The deck provides a commanding view of Monterey Bay, and the private sand area can be used when the beach is crowded or too windy.

Figure 3 shows the garden when first planted. Figure 1 shows it thirty years later with the design fulfilled. Privacy is achieved on both sides, and the garden is protected. The lines are restless and flowing, like the sea.

Northern California, 1948

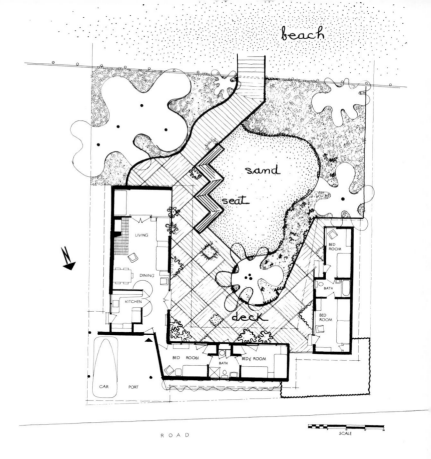

ROAD   SCALE

1   *Photograph by Michael Lau*

Photograph by Michael Laurie

Photograph by Rondal Partridge

A Garden Redesigned

In 1969 the owners of this property decided
they were ready for a change in their garden.
A swimming pool in the center was removed
and replaced with a flowing shape of lawn on
which multitrunked birch trees give shade
and pattern (Fig. 1).

An indoor pool, designed as an extension of
the house and with glass doors opening out
into the garden, was located at the side of the
property (Figs. 3 and 5).

The terrace is of brick in three shades of tan,
laid in a herringbone pattern. This treatment
gives variety to the wide hard-surface areas.

On the open north side the uninterrupted
view of the city 20 miles away is emphasized
by a projection of the terrace, a fountain,
and flanking obelisks brought from Italy (Fig.
3). Iron railings and a low wall define the
edge. Below, a path curves around the
hillside, which is planted with ground
coverings and stabilizing cotoneaster.

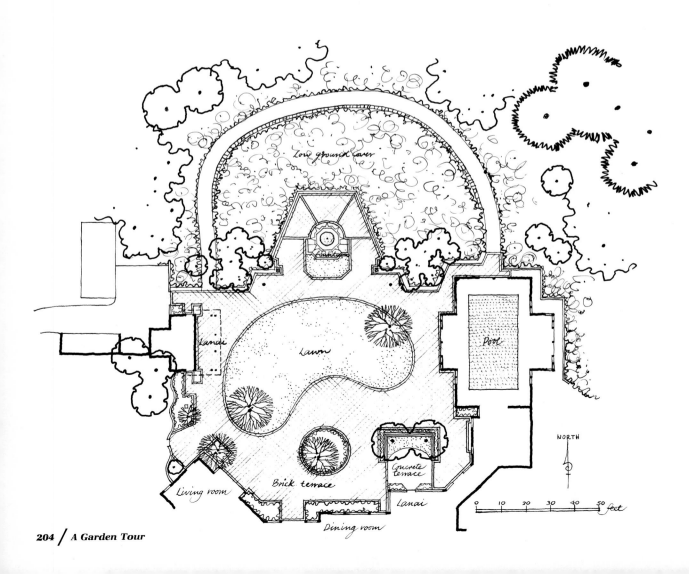

Low ground cover

Lanai

Lawn

Pool

Concrete
terrace

NORTH

Living room

Brick terrace

Lanai

0 10 20 30 40 50 feet

Dining room

Photograph by Pan-Anela Messenger

Photograph by Carolyn Caddes

The fountain, the focal point of the garden, is set in an octagonal enclosure placed on a terrazzo star and combined with a small lawn, the sides of which repeat the angular sides of the octagon. It is flanked by the Florentine obelisks and two Danish street lamps (Figs. 1 and 3).

From the new structure which houses the swimming pool (Fig. 5), one looks across the garden.

A serpentine wall, Fig. 6, built on the west side between the house and lanai, completes the enclosure of the garden. The wall was formerly painted white, but when the garden was redesigned the color was removed, and the wall now blends with the brick of the terrace and gives a fitting background for the sculpture.

A continuous wood bench encloses a U-shaped patio shaded by two La Brea elms and easily accessible from the house. This space is often used as a summer dining area (Fig. 7).

Northern California, 1968

Photograph by Carolyn Caddes

5

Photograph by Pam-Anela Messenger

A Country Garden

This is a garden designed for people who want to do a reasonable amount of controlled gardening and a generous amount of relaxing.

There is space for a border of color, a vegetable garden, a pot rack to display favorite plants, a terrace next to the house, and a swimming pool.

Behind the board-and-batten fence (which screens an undesirable view) is a garden work area with tools, potting bench, greenhouse, and storage.

The garden wraps around the carpet of lawn.

"Nothing is more pleasant to the Eye than Greene Grasse kept finely shorn."
FRANCIS BACON, *Of Gardens*, 1625

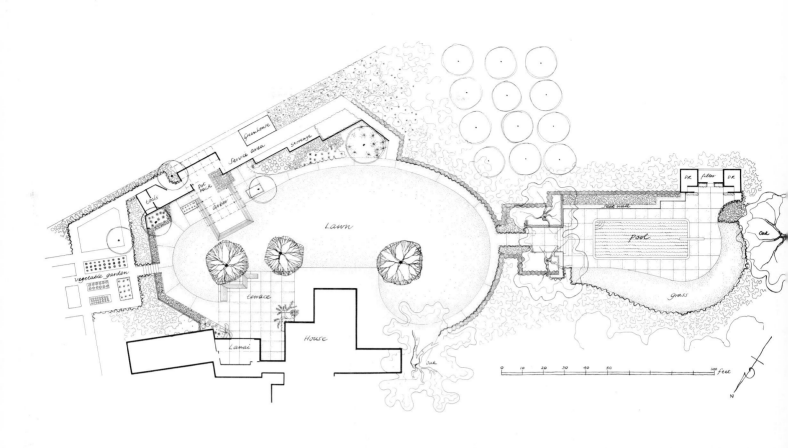

Greenhouse
Service area   Storage
Pot rack
Arbor
Tools
Lawn
vegetable garden
terrace
House
Lanai
Oak

D.R.   filter   D.R.
seat wall
Pool
grass
Oak

0   10   20   30   40   50   100 feet

N

The pot rack is in a metal arbor (Fig. 4) with
a redwood-slat roof. This was planned as a
display area which offers protection for the
owner's potted plants. Hours of relaxing work
are spent in developing plants worthy of star
billing and display. It is a colorful spot. Broad
wood steps lead to red-brown tanbark, a soft,
natural material used to contrast with the
grass green of the lawn. The zigzag form of
the bench in the foreground echoes the
stepped alignment of the fence, which is
stained alternately gray and black.

4

Photograph by Michael Laurie

otograph by Michael Laurie

A productive vegetable garden with
convenient raised beds (Fig. 6) lies hidden at
a lower level on a warm, south-facing slope.

7

The color border in this country garden is planted in hardy, long-blooming perennials with blue, yellow, and white predominating. Foliage varies from the bright green of the agapanthus to the pale yellow-green of the sedums; from the gray of the lavender and acacia to the near-white of the artemesia. There is always color, in either flower or foliage, from spring to late fall (Fig. 7).

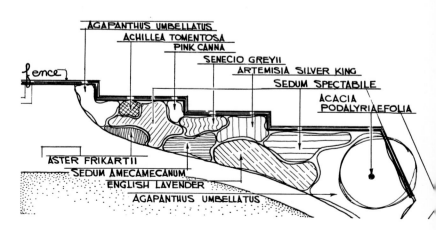

AGAPANTHUS UMBELLATUS
ACHILLEA TOMENTOSA
PINK CANNA
SENECIO GREYII
ARTEMISIA SILVER KING
SEDUM SPECTABILE
ACACIA PODALYRIAEFOLIA
fence
ASTER FRIKARTII
SEDUM AMECAMECANUM
ENGLISH LAVENDER
AGAPANTHUS UMBELLATUS

The swimming pool was added at a later date. Steps lead down to a rectangular pool surrounded by paving and grass, forming a natural clearing in the original oak woodland. The transition between the garden and nature is clearly marked by low seat walls and a precise lavender hedge.

Woodside, California, 1950

© *Photograph by Morley Baer*

A Garden in the Desert

In the warm climate of Arizona, a swimming pool was high on the list of priorities for this new house and garden. Because of the nature of the site, the only possible position was in an area exposed to strong winds. To provide protection but retain the spectacular view across the broad desert valley below, a five-panel glass screen was built in the same stuccoed masonry as the house.

Photographs by Maynard L. Parker

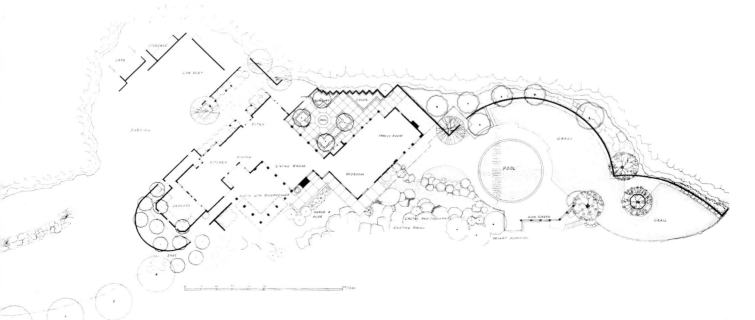

The windscreen and retaining walls emphasize the distinction between the designed garden and the surrounding rugged desert landscape.

The introduced olives suggest an oasis, while cacti and rock outcroppings are native to the site. Lights placed low give a soft illumination to the scene at night.

tographs by Maynard L. Parker

Water is essential to this garden, to suggest
coolness by both sight and sound.

Too precious to lie silent, it cools a sunny
courtyard through a fountain spouting
upward from an octagonal pool.

Arizona, 1963

Photographs by Maynard L. Parker

8 ▶

Overlooking the Golf Course

The natural beauty of this site in Santa
Barbara, within a short distance of the ocean
and cradled in the mountains, provides a
magnificent setting for the house and garden.

A spacious entrance court leads to a covered
entry walk. To the right is a small, enclosed
breakfast patio planted with lemons and
gardenias. Beyond its walls can be seen the
Santa Ynez range of mountains. The living
room and the bedrooms of the house open
on a classical, walled, paved enclosure with a
central swimming pool and twin flanking
gazebos connected to the house by a
wood-lath pergola (Fig. 3). The open gazebos
provide two additional rooms well suited to
the climate. From one, a window opens up a
view through the high wall to the golf course
(Fig. 5). This small garden provides privacy
and delight in a way reminiscent of the town
gardens of Pompeii.

Santa Barbara, California, 1971

(See also page 191.)

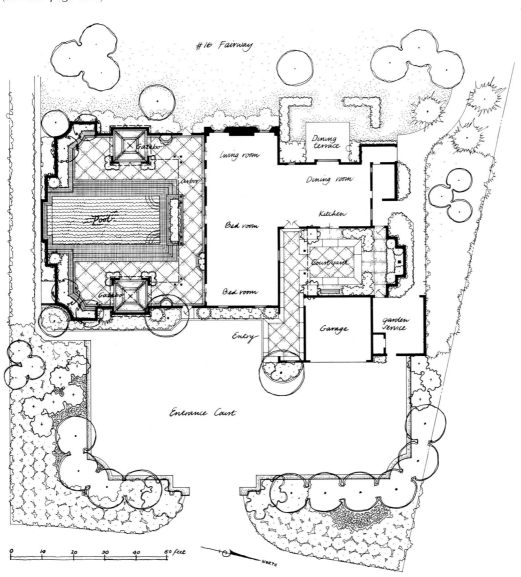

3

5

A Garden in the Fields

On a former ranch site, this house and garden were built in 1961. The owners are polo enthusiasts, and because a place for their beloved horses was a primary consideration, the original stables and meadows were retained.

To break up the expanse of the flat parking court and to create interest at the entry, a raised bed was built a car's width from the front porch, to house a clipped parterre in keeping with the French architectural style of the house. It is a formal, classical design planted with two pruned fig trees and hedges of Japanese box (Fig. 1).

On the southwest side of the house, a path winds through a small, informal garden planted with dogwood, rhododendrons, magnolias, and a variety of annuals and perennials which give bright splashes of color (Fig. 3).

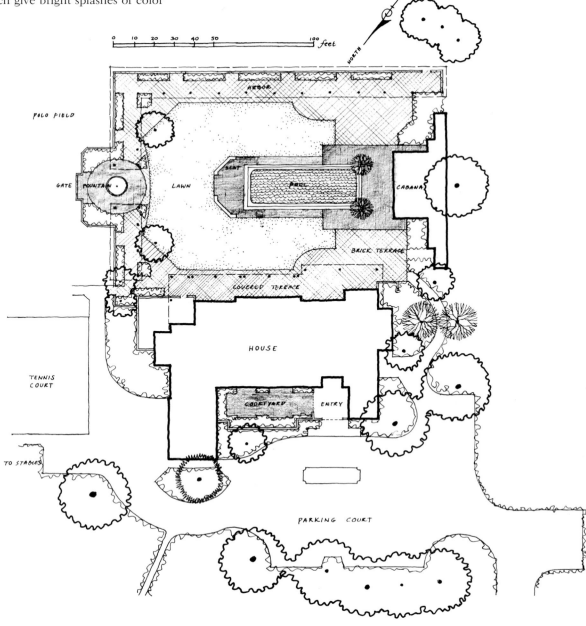

1

3

Photographs by Pam-Anela Messenger

The main garden at the back of the house is
surrounded by meadow on two sides. A
cloistered walk, which defines the boundaries
of the garden, has occasional windows of
graceful wrought-iron railings to allow
viewing of the pastures and equine friends.
Under each window is a teak bench (Figs. 4
and 5).

The central feature of the garden is a
swimming pool.

Hexagonal paving blocks were used to define
the cabana terrace and pool edge; contrasting
in form to the brick paving under the pergola
and on the terrace, at the same time they
blend in color and texture. Around the
fountain the hexagonal blocks give emphasis
to the focal point (Fig. 6).

4

5

With its continuous paved walk around the periphery and ample open space, the garden readily accommodates large groups of guests. At night, with soft lighting around the pool and pergola, flowers surrounding the water's edge, and the brick benches cushioned for seating, it is a garden used and loved for festive occasions.

Atherton, California, 1965

Photograph by Philip Fein

A Fallen Oak Influenced This Garden

Just outside the entrance-hall door is a large, fallen live oak, still growing and in good condition. One large branch arches over the garden vista, and another rests just 2 feet from the ground. Stone steps were built up and over this branch, which itself forms the top step. The oak is festooned with variegated ivy hung with baskets of fuchsias and begonias.

Along the central path, which extends to a row of magnificent Lombardy poplars, seasonal annuals are planted—nemesia in the spring, stock in the summer, Mexican zinnias in the fall and white begonias in the winter.

The boxwood, which had bordered flower beds along the old garden's wandering paths, was used to make the curving edge along the path and to border the rose-garden beds in the distance.

Hillsborough, California, 1948

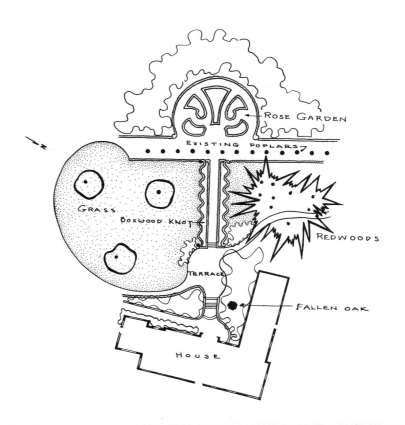

ROSE GARDEN

EXISTING POPLARS

GRASS

BOXWOOD KNOT

REDWOODS

TERRACE

FALLEN OAK

HOUSE

Next to the Golf Course

In 1959 this property was a vacant hillside,
adjacent to the golf course and surrounded
by tall eucalyptus and pine trees. A wall, up
to 8 feet in height, was built to retain the
parking court in front of the house (Fig. 1).

Once inside the entry, the glass-walled atrium
comes into view. A quatrefoil pool and
fountain, orange trees, and an Italian cypress
are seen in a shaft of sunlight (Fig. 2).
Beyond are large glass doors leading to the
terrace and garden (Fig. 4).

The transition from house to garden is
carried out by the continuation of the
terrazzo floors of the interior space onto the
floor of the terrace, the only change being
the squares of the terrace laid diagonally to
break the monotony of the expanse of
paving.

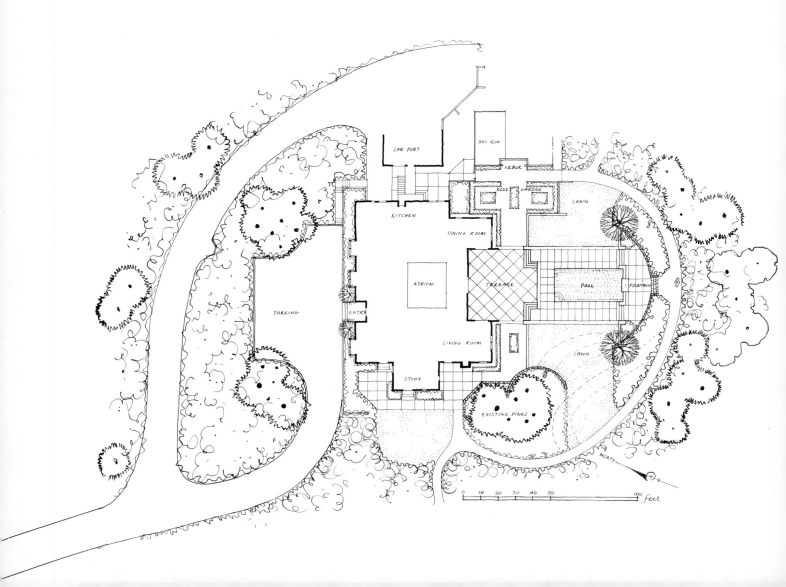

4

The main focus of the garden is the pool.
Elevated from the terrace, it resembles more
an ornamental reflecting pool than a typical
swimming pool. This effect was achieved by
eliminating the diving board and climbing
bars, sealing the pool in tan rather than
aqua, and adding an elevated fountain at the
far end. Above the fountain a series of steps
leads to the south boundary, where one's eye
focuses on an openwork sculpture (Fig. 5).

5

Photographs by Pam-Anela Messenger

When one turns to face the house, the symmetry of the garden is evident. The atrium's Italian cypress—planted before the walls of the house were constructed—can be seen emerging into the picture (Fig. 6).

The reclining figure at poolside (see also page 101) views a mass of Chinese wisteria trailing over the arbor and the magic of blossoming chestnuts and flowering crabapple (Fig. 7).

Hillsborough, California, 1959

Photographs by Pam-Anela Messenger

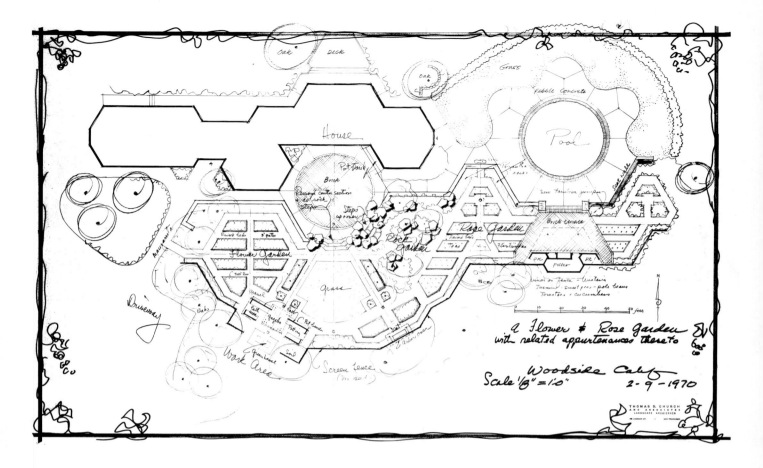

A Plant Lover's Garden

The garden design for this country house in northern California provides for the owner's serious horticultural interests. Easily cultivated raised beds for flowers, vegetables, and fruit flank a central grass panel. A gazebo and an arbor were built along the garden's edge; one conceals a lath-covered work area and greenhouse (Fig. 6); the other, with its wisteria-covered pergola, shades a seat and sculpture. Built against the far side of the gazebo and outside the fence, the lath-house is concealed when the garden is viewed from the house.

Although there is no question of being overlooked in this bucolic scene, a high fence surrounds the garden to prevent deer from walking in and enjoying its delicacies.

A concrete retaining seat wall links a brick terrace outside the living room with the swimming pool to the east.

Serpentine-edged pebble concrete paving surrounds the circular pool. On one side is a cabana whose brick terrace matches the coping around the pool. On the other side the lawn is edged with a low juniper hedge, defining the boundary and linking this part of the garden with the view of wooded landscape.

Figures 2 and 6 show the garden in winter, ten years after the first planting.

Woodside, California, 1970

2

Photograph by Carolyn Cadd

3

Photograph by Glenn Christiansen, courtesy of Sunset Magazine

4

Photographs by Carolyn Caddes

5

*Photograph by Glenn Christiansen,
courtesy of* Sunset Magazine

6

An Italian Garden in California

A long, winding driveway climbs uphill to a
spacious parking court, encircled by a
curving fieldstone retaining wall. Olive trees
in beds of ivy top the wall and assist in
preventing erosion of the steep hillside. A
yellow-green La Brea elm and a dark,
blue-green Italian cypress stand either side of
wrought-iron gates, the entry to a walled-in
courtyard (Fig. 1).

A former house had been removed from this
beautiful hilltop, and the new owners
requested that the existing grove of
magnificent Italian stone pines be featured as
a major focus of interest in their new house
and garden plan. The pines were
incorporated into the design as a setting for
the formal swimming pool around which the
garden is built. The retaining wall and terrace
form a half circle stretching toward the trees
which frame one end of the pool (Fig. 3).

Inside the gracefully fabricated iron gates, a
colonnade with evergreen grapevines trained
on the arbor leads to the entrance of the
house, a pale-ochre building which has the
air of an Italian villa built around a central
garden. Symmetrical planters border the
corners of one end of the pool, and fragrant
jasmine cascades to the water's edge (Fig. 4).

Facing the colonnade, one's eyes focus on
a recessed niche framing a ceramic plaque by
the Italian sculptor Luca della Robbia. The

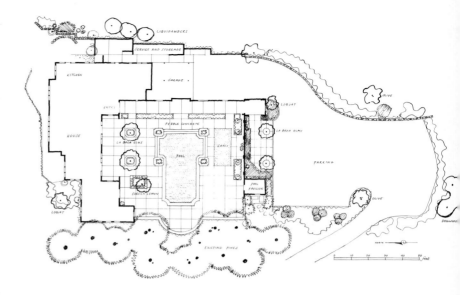

pale-blue background of the sculpture is
repeated in the color of the pool. The niche,
with a relief of lattice in a classic arch,
provides the right frame for Luca's *Madonna
and Child*, which would be otherwise lost
hanging on the bare wall of the colonnade.

Italian urns, placed on the terrace to house
marguerites and pelargoniums, together with
plant materials including olive, orange and
lemon, oleander, Chinese wisteria, and lilac,
combine to evoke a feeling of the
Mediterranean in this hilltop garden.

Northern California, 1966

Photographs by Pam-Anela Messenger

4

A Garden in the Northwest

In this garden overlooking a lake near
Tacoma, Washington, existing features, such
as the long brick walk, were retained, while
others, including the driveway and entrance
court (Fig. 1), were redesigned. The drive
approaches the house obliquely, curving
through groves of native trees and
rhododendrons. Glimpses of the house are
caught across a wide lawn.

The basic formality of the plan contrasts
attractively with the surrounding vegetation.
Formal planting beds are located on an axis
with the pool and a fine view of Mount
Ranier (Fig. 6). Woodland glades were
designed to incorporate a large collection of
rhododendrons. Since the owners are
enthusiastic gardeners, a garden room
provides an appropriate transition between
house and garden in a mild but often wet
climate. It is balanced at the far end of the
brick walk by a lattice-domed summerhouse,
with skillfully hidden dressing rooms and
kitchen (Figs. 3 and 12).

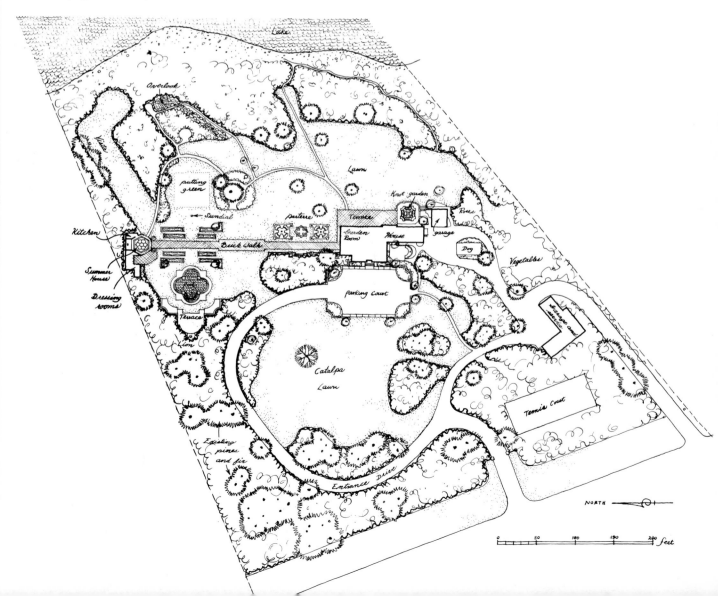

Photograph by Michael Laurie

Photograph by Charles R. Pearson

The form chosen for the pool was a
quatrefoil, in keeping with the simplicity and
elegance of the traditional garden design. Its
classic form fits easily into the existing scene,
and its 40 feet of length in two directions
keeps the swimmers happy. Divers must be
content with jumping off the flower boxes,
for a board would have been foreign to this
scene (Figs. 4 and 5).

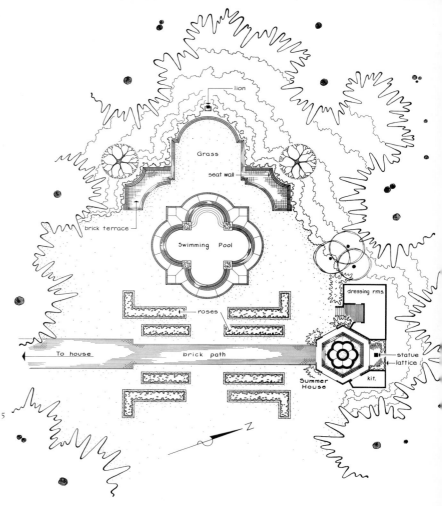

Photograph by Maynard L. Parker

The cross axis set up by the lion sculpture, the pool, and the sundial establishes a magnificent vista focused on Mount Ranier in the distance.

7

8

Adjacent to the terrace, a medieval knot garden was designed around an antique wellhead, using boxwood, germander, and gray-leaved santolina for the framework. The spaces are planted with a variety of herbs, including sweet woodruff, basil, several kinds of mint, horehound, sage, golden marjoram, French tarragon, lavender, and rosemary (Figs. 7, 8, and 9).

A decorative parterre was designed on traditional lines, with the structure planted with clipped boxwood. Seasonal flowers fill the planting areas. The whimsical topiary swans are unique and associate well with the abundant waterfowl population of the lake below (Figs. 10 and 11).

Photographs by Michael Laurie

9

Photographs by Michael Laurie

The lattice-domed summerhouse is the focal
point at the far end of the brick walk. It is
paved with a hexagonal edging of brick
surrounding a six-circled design of mosaic in
the center.

1962.

Photograph by Charles R. Pearson

A Rooftop Garden

This house and property are the same size, leaving no space for a garden. Changes had to be made, for the owners longed to feel the sunshine as well as to see it shining on the city outside their windows.

The only empty space available was the roof. Why not a garden there? It would provide fresh air, sunshine, and a place to grow plants.

Now a small garden has been built on this rooftop site. It is planted with cacti and succulents, sun lovers requiring a minimum of water, and dwarf conifers for height variation and shade. A seat wall built of wood and a narrow pathway edge this tiny retreat.

San Francisco, California, 1950

8

The Author's Garden

Thomas Church at his worktable, 1976.

Photograph by Carolyn Caddes

I've often been asked why I live in a Victorian house and why I keep it Victorian. "Why not modernize it?" people inquire. Well, I have modernized it. We have a food freezer and a clothes drier; the kitchen has a disposal, a battery of spice shelves, and two ovens. I'm working on an automatic, radar-controlled cookbook holder which will follow you from the stove to the refrigerator and back. We don't have "three dimensional spatial forces working in equal strength and in opposite directions to open our visual experience," but as soon as I find out what they are I may have them installed!

The house was built over 100 years ago, an honest expression of the taste of its time (Fig. 2). It did seem that we should accept it for what it was and remodel it in that spirit, preserve the style and add to it.

When we found the house, the garden was not run down—it did not exist! Our first garden was installed in 1933, and it has gone through many phases. With the ideas of the thirties, we did a formal, diamond-patterned, boxwood garden, with clipped tables, chairs, and peacocks. Our garden mellowed with time. The trees grew and the hedges thrived (Figs. 4 and 5).

In 1954, after many years of faithful service, the front steps fell in. The sensible thing would have been to repair some treads, clean out the dry rot, and prop the steps back up. But memories of the divided stairway at Fontainebleau haunted us and gradually became a reality. This started a chain reaction, and before it stopped we put in an entirely new garden (Fig. 6).

Now, less excitable but more enthusiastic, we have abandoned the clipped boxwood and have done a garden that is freer and more open, that lends itself to a variety of moods but is still formal in intent. It has rocks and ferns, succulents and flowers, and miscellaneous garden ornaments—a large shell for the birds, an antique Chinese goddess, a pair of Victorian urns hung with grapes, and a modern wall plaque in iron and concrete. My garden has taught me that, when you stay within the vague bounds of good taste, you can have just what you want.

1932

The year 1933 saw the garden in a formal pattern with tables, chairs, peacocks, and globes of clipped boxwood. A sloping board fence protected the garden from the street. Sycamores were planted as a screen, and a dog run was added along the side of the property.

In 1948 the formality is softened by the exuberance of plant growth. The fence is higher and level, with ivy trained in a diamond pattern. The dog run has been replaced by a new wing on the house, and elms have been planted along the entrance path.

Remodeled Three Times (Cont.)

In 1954, after twenty years, major changes
were indicated. The entrance walk now
curves to meet the new stairs, and the
planting is completely informal.

© Photograph by Morley Baer

The South Garden

Our garden life moved next door when, in the early 1940s, we acquired the adjoining property. It is less than 25 feet square, protected on all sides and reached by a stairway from the kitchen.

Whereas the front garden is primarily a blending of greens, our little south garden gives us bright color from an ever-changing number and variety of potted plants; the bright pink and red of pelargoniums, the cheerful yellow of coreopsis, the delicate pink of flowering cherry, and the white of wisteria and cyclamen.

A narrow pathway of pea gravel encircles the area, and in the center is a miniature parterre of Japanese boxwood which gives ground pattern all year round.

The South Garden (Cont.)

From the front door one looks down on a series of mini-terraces. Large palms and ferns from the Australian rain forest spread over beds of greenery. There is relatively little sun in this area, so color is primarily a blending of greens, with blue agapanthus and coral clivia and valota for a cheerful accent.

Somewhat hidden, lying in the protection of the street wall, is the only flat space. This secluded corner is a sunken garden, a small outdoor room where we can sit and reflect and where the cheerful clanging of the cable-car bell going past the gate is never obtrusive.

Photograph by Michael Lauria

We've come to the end of the tour.

If it seemed too brief, remember we had a lot of ground to cover.

If it was too long, I hope you stopped to rest.

If I've talked too much, I can only quote from Cato, who said in a letter to a friend, "Had I more time, I would have written you a shorter letter."

When your garden is finished, I hope it will be more beautiful than you had anticipated, require less care than you had expected, and have cost only a little more than you had planned.

Index